101: EVERYTHING YOU NEED TO KNOW ABOUT VODKA, GIN, RUM & TEQUILA

Bob Lipinski

Contact Information

Bob Lipinski
Website: www.boblipinski.com
E-mail: bob@hibs-usa.com
You can also find Bob on LinkedIn and FaceBook

ISBN: 1519179022
ISBN 13: 9781519179029

ABOUT THE AUTHOR

Bob Lipinski

Bob Lipinski, a Certified Sommelier (Court of Master Sommeliers), is the author of ten books and more than 500 articles. As a professional speaker, entertainer, and educator, he has conducted seminars worldwide; presentations to businesses, Fortune 500 corporations, trade shows, and conventions. He taught the Executive Staff at The White House "How-To Pair Wine with Food," "Proper Wine Service," and "Sensory Evaluation Skills." Bob also has television and radio experience as a host, writer, and guest. He has worked as a consulting *enologist* and *viticulturist*.

Bob has held executive-level sales, training, and education positions in the Wine & Spirits industry. He has also been a College Professor of Management & Marketing at N.Y. Institute of Technology; Professor of Communications, Jefferson Community College, KY;

Managing Director of Sales & Marketing U.S. Ventures Education Systems; Visiting Professor at the Culinary Institute of America; and Dean of U.S. & International Studies at the Epicurean Institute of Italy.

Bob was Vice President, National Director of Training, Brown-Forman; General Sales Manager, Premier Wine & Spirits; Director of Training Southern Wine & Spirits; National Director of Training & Wine Education, Ste. Michelle Wine Estates.

DEDICATION

To my wife Kathie, and our sons, John and Matt,
along with the many friends and colleagues I have
met along the way as we enjoyed a glass of spirits.

INTRODUCTION

Distilled spirits as we know it have been around since at least the 1100s. The first documentation of distillation took place in China, where a spirit was created from rice or possibly molasses. Countless movies have been made showing heroes and heroines consuming distilled spirits, straight, or over ice, and in a cocktail. Vodka, gin, rum, and tequila mix well with water, seltzer, cola, ginger ale, and fruit juices, as well as being a base for countless recipes and concoctions.

From the rough, high proof offerings made in years or decades past, to the modern "flavored spirits" enjoyed by the younger generation, vodka, gin, rum, and tequila have obviously evolved. Much like coffee-drinkers, it seems that every month a new style, flavor, production method, filtering regiment, and so forth is put forth, mostly through vast social media outlets.

This book presents vodka, gin, rum, and tequila as a "101 Introduction," covering the basics of each *major* category and countries of origin. In addition, I've included a section entitled "101 Things YOU Need To Know About Vodka, Gin, Rum, and Tequila."

"A dry martini. (James Bond) One. In a deep champagne goblet...Three measures of Gordon's, one of vodka, half a measure of Kina Lillet. Shake it well until it's very cold, then add a large thin slice of lemon peel. Got it?" (Ian Fleming, *Casino Royale*)

TABLE OF CONTENTS

DISTILLED SPIRITS TIME LINE

Fermented alcoholic beverages existed before distillation was understood or practiced. The origin of alcoholic beverages can be traced back to 8000 B.C., where grapes were first planted somewhere near the Black Sea. Fruits and grain were used to produce wine and beer. The first known documentation of distillation was in 1116 B.C., in China, using fermented rice. Other important chronological dates in the history of distilled spirits, wine, and brewing include the following:

_B.C._

- 2800: Egyptians used wooden barrels for storing alcoholic beverages

- 1116: First documentation of distillation taking place in China—a distilled spirit was made from fermented rice or molasses
- 1000: Alcohol, fermented from the agave plant was produced by Mexico's ancient Aztec Indians
- 800: Arak distilled from sugarcane and rice in East Indies
- 400: Hippocrates was credited with the discovery of distillation

A.D.

- 100: Greeks utilized distilling equipment
- 800: Moors learned the art of distilling from the Egyptians
- 900: Persians advanced technology of distillation
- 1200: Vodka was distilled in Poland and Russia
- 1493: Columbus brought sugarcane to the West Indies from the Canary Islands on his second voyage
- 1505: The Guild of Surgeon Barbers in Edinburgh was granted a monopoly over the manufacture of *aqua vitae,* by Royal Charter of King James IV (1488–1513)
- 1600: Rum was distilled in Barbados
- 1620: Corn spirits were common in Germany
- 1640: First distilled spirit (rum) produced in U.S. (Staten Island, New York) by William Keift, Director-General of the New Netherlands.

- 1650: Gin was distilled in Holland
- 1651: Rum was called Barbados water, rumbullion, or kill-devil (a belief that rum could cure ailments– kill the devil, so to speak)
- 1657: Rum was first produced commercially in Massachusetts
- 1725: The hydrometer was invented by John Clark, to measure amount of alcohol in solution.
- 1736: The Gin Act made gin in England prohibitively expense as a means to cut down on consumption. It was repealed in 1743.
- 1758: George Washington was elected to the Virginia House of Burgesses after distributing 75 gallons of rum to voters.
- 1769: Distillation first took place (for production of rum), in Quebec, Canada.
- 1774: Anthony Benezet, a Philadelphia Quaker published *The Mighty Destroyer Displayed*, the first full-scale assault on American drinking habits.
- 1808: The Union Temperance Society is formed in Moreau, New York
- 1810: Joseph-Louis Gay-Lussac correctly devised the overall equation for fermentation.
- 1824: Joseph-Louis Gay-Lussac developed the alcohol scale for the measurement of alcohol in solution.
- 1827: Botanist Robert Brown first studied the phenomena of irregular, random, and continuous erratic zigzag movement of minute microscopic

solid particle (colloidal) dispersions in a liquid medium. This explains why liquids rotate in a barrel, as in "barrel-aging" of wine and some distilled spirits.

- 1827: Robert Stein, a Scotsman and distiller at the Kilbagie Distillery, invented the "continuous still."
- 1830: The term "London Dry Gin" is first used for a gin made without heavy sugar syrup
- 1830: Aeneas Coffey patents the first workable "continuous still" invented in 1827, by Robert Stein.
- 1851: June 2nd; the governor of Maine signed into law a bill prohibiting the sale of alcoholic beverages.
- 1873: Tequila makes its debut in the United States, when Sauza sold three barrels to El Paso del Norte, in Texas.
- 1881: Kansas became the first state to adopt statewide Prohibition.
- 1891: United States law required the country of origin to be predominantly displayed on a product's label.
- 1902: The Blue Agave, a variety of the genus plant *Agave Tequilana Weber,* was named by Franz Weber, a German botanist, from earlier work begun in 1896.

- 1904: Michael J. Owen (1859–1923), supervisor at the Toledo Glass Factory in Toledo, Ohio, patented the Bottle Making Machine.
- 1919: On October 28, the Volstead Act was passed.
- 1920: National Prohibition began in the United States. More than 100 wineries continued limited production under government permits, making sacramental, medicinal and salted cooking wines.
- 1933: The 21st Amendment to the Constitution passed, repealing Prohibition.
- 1935: FAA (Federal Alcohol Administration) Act intended to promote fair competition in the marketing of alcoholic beverages by prohibiting certain trade practices that result in the exclusion of competing products in interstate commerce. Among other things, it also regulated the labeling and advertising practices of the alcoholic beverage industry.

"The sandwiches came and I ate three and drank a couple more martinis. I had never tasted anything so cool and clean. They made me feel civilized." (Ernest Hemingway, 1899–1961, American author, Frederic Henry in *A Farewell To Arms*, 1929)

DEFINITIONS & TERMINOLOGY

"Why don't you get out of that wet coat and into a dry martini?" (Robert Benchley to Ginger Rogers, *The Major and the Minor, 1942*). However, Robert Benchley attributed that line to his friend Charles Butterworth in the 1937 movie, "Every Day's A Holiday," where Butterworth said to actress Mae West, "You ought to get out of those wet clothes and into a dry martini."

Clear Spirits
Term often used to describe those distilled spirits that are clear in color and usually not aged in wood. These distilled spirits lack the distinctive flavor generally associated with whiskey and are *perceived* as being lighter by most consumers. Examples are Vodka (Aquavit, Schnapps), Gin (Genever), Rum (Cachaça), and Tequila

(Mezcal, Bacanora, Sotol, and Tlahuelompa). Clear spirits are also known as *white goods* and *white spirits*.

Liquor

A U.S. term commonly taken to mean distilled spirits; beverages that contain at least 40 percent alcohol (80 proof). Liquor is also known as *hard liquor* (United States) and *liquore* (Italy).

Alcoholic Beverage

As defined by U.S. Standards of Identity, any beverage in liquid form that contains not less than one-half of one percent (0.5 percent) of ethyl alcohol (ethanol) by volume and is intended for human consumption. These beverages are classified by their method of production:

Age

Period of storage of spirits in oak barrels, after distillation and before bottling, to develop character and palatability.

For most American whiskies, it means storage in new, charred oak barrels. The exceptions are corn and light whiskies, which may be aged in uncharred, new or charred, reused oak barrels. Other whiskies and brandies are generally aged in used oak barrels, whereas rum and tequila are occasionally aged in used barrels. Age may not be designated for gin or vodka. According to the United States government standards of identity, the time a whiskey spends outside of an oak barrel does not add to its age.

An "Indication of Age"

When there is an age stated on the bottle label of a distilled spirit (12, 15, 18, 21, 25, and so forth), it identifies the youngest spirit in the blend. This is for Rum, Bourbon, Canadian, Irish, Japanese, Rye, Scotch, and others. The other distilled spirits are matured for longer periods. If the spirit were for example all 12-year-old, then it would considered a "vintage-dated" spirit.

Ardent Spirits

A formerly used name for distilled spirits, dating back to at least the 1790s.

Artisanal

Term usually associated with small production distilled spirits.

Blending Spirits

Mixing various similar distilled spirits, by a distiller, to produce a uniform combination of higher quality and complexity than any one ingredient.

Still

An apparatus used to concentrate and produce distilled spirits, which are classified by the method of introducing a fermented mixture. There are two types of stills used; the pot still and the continuous still.

Continuous Still

The continuous still is often referred to as a column still, Coffey still, and patent still. The continuous still provides a continuous inflow of distilling liquid, which greatly boosts volume while saving considerable time. It generally does not produce the same high quality as the pot still.

In 1827, Robert Stein, a distiller at the Kilbagie Distillery, invented and put into production a still, which successfully distilled a continuous flow of fermented beer into a distilled spirit. Stein's still was demonstrated before the Excise authorities at Wandsworth in London, and a Dublin Excise officer called Aeneas Coffey received details of the design and further updated to the twin-column design, and received a patent for it in 1830. Prior to that, all distillations took place in *pot stills*.

Pot Still

The pot still resembles a large copper (or stainless steel) pot or kettle with a broad rounded base, topped by a long column. Copper removes unwanted sulfides and is resistant to acidity. The shape and size of the still, even the way it is fired (flame or steam), the speed of heating the liquid, the temperature of the still, and the volume of the *heart* are believed to affect the quality of the distillate. Over the years, each distillery has been reluctant to change the shape of its stills. As they wear out, they are replaced by new ones of the same design. If the last still was dented, the distillery may get the same depression hammered into the new still.

- **Hearts**: In distillation, elements that vaporize between the *heads* and *tails* and are utilized in the final product.
- **Heads**: In distillation, the first crude spirit to appear from the still; it is collected and redistilled. Heads are detected as a harsh, burning sensation in the nose and back of the throat.
- **Tails**: In distillation, the last run of a distillate; it contains a high percent of congeners (impurities) which are not used but rather are collected and redistilled.

Initially the liquid to be distilled is loaded into the base of the pot still. The liquid is then heated and kept simmering until the alcohol is vaporized and rises up into the column, taking with it flavors from the base liquid; this gives the distillate its characteristic aroma and taste. When the vapor rises to a certain point in the column, it comes into contact with a cold condenser, which turns the vapor into liquid alcohol. Pot stills produce only single batches of distilled spirits. After each batch has been distilled, the pot still must be refilled. Pot stills produce the finest quality as well as the highest priced distilled spirits, but the process is laborious and time-consuming.

The term *Proof* on a bottle of spirits

Proof is an old English term that was once called *gunpowder proof.* To test the strength of the distilled spirit, old-time distillers mixed it with gunpowder or black powder and struck a match. If it exploded or *blazed up,* it was *over proof,* too strong, and thought to be lethal. If it did not burn well or barely ignited, it was too high in water. If the distilled spirit burned slowly with a blue flame, it was considered *proof* that it contained the proper ratio of water to alcohol. Mixing 50 percent alcohol with 50 percent water gave a slow, steady flame. That strength was considered perfect and was called *100 proof.*

When physical methods for determining alcohol percentage were developed, *proof* was found to be slightly over 50 percent alcohol. Nowadays, the same scale is applied to the alcoholic content of distilled spirits on the following basis: pure 100 percent alcohol (at 60°F.) is 200 proof; 1 degree of proof is equal to 0.5 percent alcohol.

Since the repeal of Prohibition, the requirement that labels state alcohol content (formerly expressed in degrees of proof) has remained unchanged. Proof is a traditional term for alcohol content (equal to twice the percentage by volume). Thus, 80 proof means 40 percent alcohol by volume, 100 proof means 50 percent alcohol by volume, and so on.

In order to provide the consumer with clearer and more useful information on labels for distilled spirits, the United States Alcohol and Tobacco Tax and Trade Bureau (ATTTB) began to issue regulations (November 10, 1986) for labeling. Alcohol content must be indicated by percentage—not just in proof. This is a more readily understood way to convey alcohol content to the purchaser.

According to the 1986 BATF regulations, labels must show percentage by volume of alcohol, but both forms (proof and percentage) may be used. If a proof statement is used, it must be shown in direct conjunction with the percent by volume, emphasizing the fact that both expressions mean the same thing. Proof is also known in the United States as *flame up*.

"Bulk Bottling" of Spirits
Distilled spirits that have not been bottled at the distillery, but rather shipped out of the country for bottling. This saves considerable cost and in some instances, results in a fresher product. Some examples are Canadian Whisky, Blended Scotch Whisky, and *mixto* Tequila. Also referred to as *U.S. Bulk Bottling*.

"I never go jogging, it makes me spill my martini." (George Burns 1896–1996, U.S. actor and comedian)

PROHIBITION, MOONSHINE,
& RELATED TERMS

"**P**rohibition makes you want to cry into your beer and denies you the beer to cry into." (Don Marquis, 1878–1937, American writer, novelist, and playwright)

Prohibition
A law that forbade "the manufacture, sale, or transportation of intoxicating liquors within, the importation thereof into, or exportation thereof from the United States and all territory subject to the jurisdiction thereof for beverage purposes." Both Houses of Congress passed the Eighteenth Amendment on December 5, 1917. However, it was not until January 16, 1919 that the necessary three-quarters of the states ratified

the Amendment. The Eighteenth Amendment to the Constitution of the United States went into effect on January 16, 1920 (during the administration of President Woodrow Wilson, 1913–1921), and was repealed on Tuesday, December 5, 1933 (during the administration of President Franklin D. Roosevelt, 1933–1945), by the Twenty-first Amendment, which was signed at 6:55 P.M. It lasted 13 years, ten months, 19 days, 17 hours, and 32-1/2 minutes and was referred to by President Herbert Hoover (1874–1964) as "The Noble Experiment."

The *Volstead Act* of 1919, named after Andrew J. Volstead (1860–1947), a Minnesota representative (author of the Eighteenth Amendment) defined what constitutes an alcoholic beverage. Intoxicating beverages according to the Volstead Act (which took effect on October 28) were defined as those containing 0.5 percent or more alcohol by volume and fit for use for beverage purposes. It did not actually however, prohibit the consumption of alcoholic beverages. In fact, the Volstead Act—Section 29, provided for certain exemptions, including wine for sacramental purposes, homemade wine, salted wines for cooking, and liquor for medicinal and certain nonbeverage purposes, such as toilet preparations. Due to the lobbying efforts of the Virginia apple farmers, Section 29 of the Volstead Act allowed for up to 200 gallons of *non-intoxicating* cider and fruit juices to be made in the home.

Other prohibitions included 1736 to 1743, the Gin Act or Gin Prohibition was put into enforcement in

England. From 1735 to 1742, in the state of Georgia, a prohibition against "hard liquor" (distilled spirits) was imposed. From 1908 to 1934 (26 years), there was a prohibition against drinking in Iceland, it is considered the longest in modern time. From 1910 to 1919, there was a prohibition against drinking in New Zealand. From 1914 to 1924, there was a prohibition against drinking in Russia. Also known as the *Volstead Act*.

Barrel Dogging

A seldom-used moonshining operation where wooden barrels (formerly utilized by legal distilleries) are disassembled and steamed or sweated in order to capture any residual Bourbon that soaked into the wood during aging.

Bathtub Gin

An illicit alcoholic beverage made in the United States during Prohibition by mixing together neutral spirits, glycerin, and extracts or oils of juniper berries inside a bathtub. After being stirred with an oar, it was bottled and either sold or consumed. The bathtub was not only a large enough vessel to handle all the ingredients and allow stirring, but also provided a means of quickly "washing down the drain" all evidence of the concoction, in the event of a police raid.

Blind Pig

An establishment similar to a "speakeasy," except it was a low class dive.

Blockader
Slang term for one engaged in the transportation or possible sale of non-tax-paid distilled spirits.

Bootlegger
The practice of concealing *hip flasks* of alcohol in the legs of boots. It is believed that the term *bootleg* originated during the Civil War, when soldiers would sneak liquor into army camps by concealing pint bottles within their boots or beneath their trouser legs. In the United States, it was a practice of stagecoach travelers to conceal a pint-sized, flat bottle of thick glass in their boot, to have refilled at taverns along their way. It was also a way to secrete bottles of distilled spirits for later illegal sale to the Indians. The term found its way into the lingo during Prohibition as a smuggler or dealer in illegal spirits.

Drappin' The Bead
Slang moonshiners' term for mixing high-proof alcohol with very low proof alcohol or water to lower the proof strength.

Drugstore Alcohol
During Prohibition, prescriptions for alcohol as "medicine" were legal and because of this, doctors became very popular. Along with doctors, the drugstores' popularity also grew.

Granny Fee

Payoff money to law-enforcement officers as a bribe to ensure silence and cooperation in allowing a moonshiner to continue his illicit business unmolested. It was derived from the fees that midwives used to charge for delivering babies.

Grease Spots

A location where you met during Prohibition where *granny fees* (financial payoffs) were made to ensure the movement of untaxed spirits from one town to another.

Hip Flask

A slender, flat-sided container made of metal, generally for holding distilled spirits. The shape made it easy to easily insert in one's hip pocket and keep out of sight during Prohibition.

Hooch

A home-concocted drink made of boiled ferns and flour by the Alaskan Indians of the Hutsnuwu tribe, who called it *hoochinoo*. Soldiers who were sent from the United States to Alaska after the territory was purchased from Russia in 1867 added molasses and distilled it, shortening the name to *hooch*. Hooch was the Army's term for distilled spirits during the first and second World Wars. Hooch is also spelled *hootch* (United States).

Jake
A highly alcoholic (70 to 80 percent alcohol) beverage derived from Jamaican ginger produced and sold during Prohibition mostly in the south as a medicine.

Liquor Grocery
A term dating back to Prohibition for a back room liquor distributor, which dispensed liquor by the bottle or individual drink.

Moonshine
A homemade distilled product made from virtually any ingredients, which is extremely high in alcohol and quite rough. It was originally from the southern part of the United States. Moonshine is also a group of non-tax-paid distilled spirits that are sold illicitly. The word *moon* refers to it being made by the light of the moon in secret hideouts.

As early as 1796, white brandy smuggled on the coasts of Kent and Sussex, England, and gin smuggled on the north of Yorkshire were known as *moonshine*. Brought to the United States by immigrants from the British Isles, the term came into general usage with the passing of the years and the spread of the illicit distiller's art. Also known in the United States as *shine* or *white lightning*.

Moonshiner
One who produces *moonshine*.

NASCAR (National Association for Stock Car Auto Racing)

A racing organization *officially* formed on February 21, 1948. Stock car racing has its origins during Prohibition, when drivers ran *bootleg whiskey* made primarily in the Appalachian region of the United States. Bootleggers needed to distribute their illicit products and typically, they used small, fast vehicles designed to out-run federal agents. Many of the drivers would modify their cars for speed and handling, as well as increased cargo capacity, and some of them came to love the fast-paced driving down twisted mountain roads.

The repeal of Prohibition in 1933 dried up some of their business, but by then Southerners had developed a taste for moonshine, and some of the drivers continued *runnin' shine*, this time evading the *revenuers* who were attempting to tax their operations. These drivers continued to *soup up* their stock cars. Bootleggers used to hold races on Sundays to determine who had the fastest car. In addition to a supercharged engine, moonshiners also installed heavy shocks and springs in their cars so that when they were carrying a heavy load of Mason jars full of liquor, the car would not sag. The cars continued to improve and by the late 1940s, races featuring these cars were being run for pride and profit. These races were popular entertainment in the rural Southern United States and they are most closely associated with Wilkes County region of North Carolina.

Raines Law
In 1896, in New York, there was a Sabbath Law named after Senator John Raines, author of the bill, which prohibited the sale of alcoholic beverages on Sunday except in hotels and to guests only.

Revenuers
The Alcohol Tax Unit men who enforced taxation of alcoholic beverages during Prohibition.

Runner
A person or persons who transport illicitly made (moonshine) distilled spirits to another person or location.

Speakeasy
A term applied to illicit saloons in New York City in 1899 (which predated Prohibition). Speakeasies served alcoholic beverages only to persons who would appear at the door and softly speak the password in order to enter. In certain parts of the country, a saloonkeeper would charge customers to see an attraction (such as an animal act), and provide a "complimentary" alcoholic beverage, thus circumventing the law. Also, an old Irish term for a place where illicit whiskey was sold. Also known in the United States as *Blind Pig*, *Blind Tiger*, *Booze Can*, and *Gin Joint*.

Sweet Lightnin'
Moonshine that has honey, maple syrup, or other sugary substances added to help make it palatable.

Teedum Barrel

Barrel or other storage vessel where moonshiners kept their private drinking liquor. The term also applies to craft whiskey distillers for their personal consumption.

The Bible Belt

The southern Bible Belt was described by the late Will Rogers as those states where citizens "stagger to the polls to vote dry." These are the last tottering strongholds of the professional Prohibitionists and their allies, the old moonshiners of the Blue Ridge and Great Smoky Mountains. As late as 1981, almost one-third of the counties in the South were legally *dry* (more than a third in Alabama, Georgia, Kentucky, and Mississippi and more than half in Tennessee). *See* Dry County.

The Real McCoy

An expression that derives its name from (William Frederick McCoy, 1877–1948) Captain Bill McCoy, a Florida boat maker who built yachts for Andrew Carnegie and the Vanderbilt's. During Prohibition (1920–1933), he ran *rum row* and Scotch whisky consignments from Nassau in the Bahamas to the Florida coast or north to Long Island. The distilled spirits were sold just outside the United States' territorial waters from his tall ship, the *Arethusa*, to motor launches and other vessels. He was a man of integrity who shipped to the United States nothing but *genuine* spirits The reputation of his rum, Irish, and Scotch whisky was so high (because he never *cut* them with distilled water) that the expression The *Real McCoy* became a byword for quality. Francis Berry (Berry Brothers Distillers of England) traveled to Nassau, where large consignments of spirits were bonded, prior to dispatch to South America and, illegally, into the United States. In Nassau Berry met and appointed as his agent Captain William McCoy to bring *Cutty Sark* Scotch whisky into the United States.

"I never should have switched from Scotch to Martinis." (Humphrey Bogart, 1899–1957, American film actor)

OTHER TERMS

"I like to have a martini, two at the very most. After three I'm under the table, after four I'm under my host!" (Dorothy Parker, 1893–1967, American writer and humorist)

Booze

The first reference of the word *booze*, meaning "alcoholic drink," appears in the English language around the fourteenth century as *bouse*. The spelling we use today didn't appear until the seventeenth century. A more popular story mistakenly credited E. G. Booz, a distiller in Philadelphia. From 1840 until 1870, Booz used to bottle and sell whiskey under the name of "E. G. Booz's Old Cabin Whiskey," which he bought in barrels. Booz put his name, address, and date of purchase on each of his bottles, which were shaped like little log cabins, from the Whitney Glass Works, in Philadelphia. However, he stopped this practice because the handmade bottles became too expensive.

In addition, it's a song ("Mr. Booze") from Robin and The 7 Hoods (1964), sung by Bing Crosby and starring Rat Pack members (Dean Martin, Frank Sinatra, and Sammy Davis, Jr.).

Dry County
County (or similar governmental jurisdiction) in the United States whose voters have not approved the sale of alcoholic beverages. Counties permitting sale only by private clubs are considered dry. It is basically a continuation of Prohibition for that county. *See* Wet County.

Wet County
County (or similar governmental jurisdiction) in the United States permitting the sale of alcoholic beverages by the drink (on-premise) and by package (off-premise), or by package only. Under this definition, counties can have private clubs or unlicensed outlets selling distilled spirits and still be considered legally dry for distilled spirits, or a wet county could be without a distilled spirit outlet. *See* Dry County.

Dutch Courage
A term given to gin by British soldiers, returning from the Eighty Years War (1568–1648) in the Low Countries

in the Netherlands, who sampled the juniper-flavored distilled spirit (genever) and nicknamed it *Dutch Courage.* Also known as *Hollands.*

Flute
Slang term for a soda bottled filled with whiskey or other distilled spirits.

Rummy
An old slang term (USA) for a person who drinks too much alcohol.

White Dog
The clear, white distillate after the second distillation, prior to barrel aging in the making of American (Bourbon and Rye) Whiskey.

"During prohibition W. C. Fields was asked why, if he didn't have a drinking problem, did he buy 300 cases of gin before it started. He replied, I didn't think it would last that long."

SERVING "CLEAR SPIRITS"

"**M**odern Jazz, Brigitte Bardot, and Vodka." (Pablo Picasso, was asked to name the three most important features of post-war French culture)

What does served "Neat" mean?
Distilled spirits (generally whiskey) that are served "straight" from the bottle without ice, seltzer, water, mixes, and so forth. The term "straight" is British or Irish and can be traced back to the 1570s, where *neat* or pure spirits were offered to one's friends or family members. Neat is also known as *dram* (Scotland) and *shot* (United States).

What is a "Back?"
A glass of chilled water or carbonated water generally served to accompany a distilled spirit, upon request.

What is a "Chaser?"

Slang term for water, seltzer, or even a glass of beer that is drunk immediately after consuming a shot of neat or unmixed distilled spirits. The term has been used since the 1890s.

What does "Straight Up" mean?

A cocktail that is strained and served *up off the ice* in a stemware glass. Some examples are the martini, the Manhattan, and sours. Straight up is also known as *up* (United States).

"He who has not been at a tavern knows not what a paradise it is." (Pietro Aretino, 1492–1556, Italian writer and poet)

"CLEAR SPIRITS" COCKTAILS & TOOLS

"**I** never have more than one drink before dinner," said Bond. "But I do like that one to be very large and very strong and very cold and very well-made." (James Bond, *Casino Royale* "*When referring to a martini*")

Alabama Slammer

A cocktail consisting of Southern Comfort, amaretto, sloe gin, and orange juice, made popular in the early 1980s.

Bacardi

A cocktail containing Bacardi rum, grenadine syrup, sugar, and lime juice. In addition, Bacardi is a brand name of a rum originally produced in Cuba, now made in Puerto Rico. In 1936, the New York Supreme Court ruled that a "Bacardi Cocktail is not a Bacardi Cocktail unless made with Bacardi Rum."

Banana Cow
A cocktail created by Trader Vic, consisting of a banana, sugar syrup, milk, rum, bitters, and vanilla extract.

Black Russian
A cocktail consisting of vodka and Kahlúa. The drink was purportedly made in 1949, by Gustave Tops, bartender at the Metropolitan Hotel, in Brussels. Tops created the drink in honor of Perle Mesta, U.S. ambassador to Luxembourg, a frequent patron. The name of the drink is allegedly a reference to the Cold War between Russia and much of Europe; so Tops mixed Russian vodka with a black coffee liqueur.

Bloody Mary
A cocktail created by Ferdinand Petiot, a bartender at Harry's Bar in Paris in the 1920s. It was named after Queen Mary I of England (1516–1558) who, because of her persecution of Protestants, attained the nickname Bloody Mary. It was later called a *Bucket of Blood*, after a nightclub in Chicago, then *Red Snapper,* and *Morning Glory.* It was introduced into the United States in the 1930s. It consists of vodka, Tabasco sauce, Worcestershire sauce, tomato juice, lemon juice, salt, and pepper and is often considered a remedy for a hangover.

Blue Hawaii

A cocktail consisting of rum, blue curaçao, pineapple juice, and sour mix. It was invented in 1957 by legendary bartender Harry Yee, at the Hilton Hawaiian Village, in Waikiki, Hawaii.

Blue Lagoon

A cocktail consisting of vodka, blue curaçao, and lemon juice, which was created at Harry's New York Bar in Paris in 1960, by Andrew MacElhone, son of the original owner, Harry MacElhone.

Bounce

A cocktail popular in colonial days, consisting of rum, whiskey, or brandy poured over cherries, with sugar, and spices (cinnamon, cloves, or nutmeg), added.

Bronx Cocktail

A cocktail consisting of gin, sweet and dry vermouth, and orange juice. It was created by Johnnie Solon, a bartender at the Waldorf-Astoria Hotel in New York City, in the 1930s. Supposedly, the cocktail was named after the Bronx Zoo.

Bullshot

A cocktail consisting of vodka, beef broth, Tabasco sauce, Worcestershire sauce, celery salt and black pepper. The drink originated at the Caucus Club Restaurant in

Detroit, Michigan in the 1960s, by owner Lester Gruber, and a representative from a local soup company.

Caipiriñha
A cocktail consisting of cachaça (a rum distilled from sugarcane), lime wedges, and sugar.

Calibogus
A beverage of rum, spruce beer, and molasses, typically served warm. Supposedly, it was popular with colonial-era sailors in New England. Variation in spelling are *calabogus, calibougas,* and *caliboque,* among others.

Cape Codder
A cocktail consisting of vodka and cranberry juice, named after Cape Cod, Massachusetts. The drink was conceived in 1945, by the Ocean Spray cranberry growers' cooperative under the name "Red Devil." The "Cape Codder" name dates from the early 1960s.

Champoreau
Hot black coffee that is drunk with the addition of grape or fruit brandy, rum, or even red wine. It was first served to the French soldiers while serving in Algeria (1830–1962).

Charka
A drinking vessel containing about five ounces. The word *charka* means vodka or tot cup, which has a

centuries old tradition in the Russian culture. It is also an old vodka measure, first appearing in the sixteenth century. As a result of a nineteenth century decree, the measure was reduced to slightly more than four ounces.

Chi Chi
A cocktail popularized in the 1970s, consisting of vodka, coconut cream, pineapple juice, and garnished with mint leaves, pineapple chunks, maraschino cherry, or orange slice.

Christy Girl
A cocktail consisting of gin, peach brandy, grenadine, and an egg white. It originated at the Howard Chandler Christy Room of New York's Sherry-Netherlands Hotel. Howard Chandler Christy (1873–1952) was a prominent illustrator and often sought-out portrait painter. His illustration of the American girl, a perky, outdoors woman, gave name to this cocktail.

Copacabana
A cocktail consisting of coffee-flavored brandy, light rum, white crème de cacao, and lemon juice.

Cosmopolitan
A cocktail consisting of vodka, triple sec, cranberry juice and freshly squeezed lime juice. Its origin is unknown

with conflicting dates, locations and people who supposedly first made this cocktail.

Cuba Libre

On December 10, 1898, the Spanish-American War to free Cuba from Spain, ended with the signing of the Treaty of Paris, thereby giving Cuba its independence. During the earlier days of fighting, Teddy Roosevelt's Rough Riders (who captured San Juan Hill on July 11), also helped establish rum into the United States with a drink named the *Cuba Libre*. An unknown U.S. Army officer who mixed rum with his daily ration of Coca-Cola named the drink. The drink is known in the United States as *rum and coke.*

Daiquiri

A cocktail invented in or about 1898 by Jennings S. Cox, an American, who served as chief engineer for the Spanish-American Iron Company, near the village of Daiquiri in Cuba. It is said to have originated at the Venus Bar in Santiago de Cuba and was named after the copper mines that Cox supervised. A daiquiri is made with light rum, sugar, and lime juice.

Dog's Nose

An eighteenth century cocktail consisting of warm stout laced with gin and flavored with sugar and nutmeg. The drink is supposedly named because it's wet and black and is said to be a favorite drink of Charles Dickens. The cocktails appears in the Pickwick Papers, by Charles Dickens, 1836–1837.

Eggnog
A rich, creamy, nonalcoholic dairy beverage made with egg yolks, cream, and sugar and generally served during cold weather. The alcoholic version includes brandy or rum as well. The word *eggnog*, first used around 1775, is probably a corruption of "Egg-and-Grog." Also spelled *egg nog*.

Flip
A popular drink in the United States during the early 1700s. It was made by combining rum, beer, cream, beaten eggs, and various spices, which were then heated by plunging a loggerhead into the mixture, causing it to foam (or *flip*) and take on a burnt, bitter flavor. Flip is also known as *beer flip* (United States).

Gibson
A cocktail consisting of gin or vodka, white dry vermouth, and garnished with a pearl cocktail onion. The drink was apparently named after the American illustrator Charles Dana Gibson (1867–1944), famous for his drawings of the turn-of-the-century *Gibson Girl*. His main model was his wife, Irene Langhorne. (Her sister, was the famous Lady Astor.) The two cocktail onions

are believed to represent her breasts. The story goes that Gibson ordered a martini—usually served with an olive—from the bartender Charley Connolly of the Players Club in New York City. Connolly found himself out of olives and instead served the drink with two small white onions. The cocktail is first mentioned in print in 1904.

Gimlet

A cocktail consisting of gin and Rose's Lime Juice. In 1867, the Merchant Shipping Act was passed, whereby all vessels, Royal Navy and Merchant, were required to carry lime juice for a daily ration to ships' passengers. The concern was *scurvy*, caused by a deficiency of vitamin C, which had been the scourge of sailors since the early days of sailing ships. This enactment resulted in British sailors being called *limeys*. Rear-Admiral Sir Thomas Desmond Gimlette (1857–1943), who served in the Royal Navy as a surgeon (from 1879 to 1917), wanted to make the lime juice more palatable, so he diluted it with gin (before that, rum was used) and unintentionally created a new drink. Although this is a credible story, it is not substantiated in his obituary in the London Times, October 6, 1943.

Gin and It

An abbreviation for Gin and *Italian* sweet red vermouth, a cocktail popularized between the 1930s and 1960s.

Gin and Tonic

A cocktail consisting of gin and sparkling tonic water, supposedly created around 1852.

Gin Fizz

A cocktail consisting of gin, lemon juice, and sugar, and topped with seltzer, supposedly created in the late 1880s.

Godmother

A cocktail consisting of amaretto and vodka.

Harvey Wallbanger

A cocktail believed to be concocted in 1969, consisting of orange juice, vodka, and Galliano liqueur. It seems that in southern California (according to legend), Tom Harvey would arrive at the Duke's Blackwatch Bar on Sunset Boulevard in Hollywood, after a day's surfing and order an *Italian Screwdriver*; then, after consuming several of them, he would attempt to leave and start banging into walls! Hence the name.

Credit for the cocktail is sometimes given to Donato "Duke" Antone, a bartender, who reportedly created this concoction while living in southern California. However, there is debate as to its credibility.

However, another, more plausible story is about George Bednar, who in 1966 became marketing director of McKesson Import Co., an importing company that represented Galliano Liqueur. It seems George somehow "discovered" a recipe from the 1950s, and re-christened it along with that fateful surfer, Tom Harvey. The figure of Harvey Wallbanger was supposedly designed by commercial artist Bill Young, upon request of McKesson.

Hot Buttered Rum
A cocktail consisting of dark rum, brown sugar, cloves, butter, and boiling water, dating back to the 1650s in New England.

Hurricane
A cocktail consisting of dark rum, passion fruit, grenadine, and various citrus juices. The cocktail was created in the 1940s by Pat O'Brien, proprietor of *Pat O'Brien's Bar*, located at 718 St. Peter Street, in New Orleans.

John Collins
A cocktail consisting of whiskey, lemon juice, sugar, and soda water. John Collins, the headwaiter waiter at the Limmer's Hotel and Coffee House on Conduit Street in London created the drink in the mid-1800s. He originally made the cocktail with *genever* (gin). *See* Tom Collins.

Kamikaze
A cocktail consisting of vodka, triple sec, and lime juice. It was supposedly created in 1972 by Tony Lauriano, bartender at Les Pyrénées Restaurant in New York, to

honor the Broadway show Jesus Christ Superstar. The name supposedly derived from the Japanese term, meaning *divine wind*, for the Japanese pilots of the last years of World War II, who would commit suicide by crashing their planes into American ships; metaphorically, drinking one such cocktail would be committing a suicidal act.

Loggerhead
A long-handled tool with a ball or bulb at the end, which is heated and plunged into drinks, making them hiss and steam. It was often used to heat beer or rum-based drinks.

Long Island Iced Tea
A drink created in the late 1970s by Robert "Rosebud" Butt, bartender at the Oak Beach Inn (OBI), in Hampton Bays, Long Island, New York. It consists of gin, light rum, tequila, vodka, triple sec, lemon juice, and a splash of Coke or Pepsi.

Mai Tai
A cocktail consisting of light rum, dark rum, orgeat syrup, triple sec, pineapple juice, grenadine syrup, and lime juice. This world-famous drink created in 1944 by Victor "Trader Vic" Bergeron at his bar in Emeryville, Oakland, California, is translated from Tahitian to mean *out of this world, the best.*

Margarita

A cocktail consisting of Tequila, triple sec, and freshly squeezed lime juice, with the rim of the glass coated with coarse salt. There are many stories as to the origin of the Margarita cocktail. One story states that Danny Negrete, the manager at the Garci Crespo Hotel in Puebla created it for his girlfriend in 1936. Others believe it was created in 1938, in Rosarito Beach, Tijuana and named after showgirl Marjorie King, who was allergic to all types of distilled spirits except Tequila. Danny (Carlos) Herrera, the bartender kept inventing new and exciting ways to serve Tequila so Marjorie would not be bored. Another story states it created by a Virginia City bartender in memory of his girlfriend who was accidentally shot during a barroom brawl. A further legend places the birth of this cocktail in 1940s Hollywood by Enrique Bastante Gutierrez, a former cocktail champion who mixed drinks for some of the world's most famous film stars. Apparently, actress Rita Hayworth (whose real name was Margarita Carmen Cansino) was one of his loyal customers and he invented the drink especially for her. Another version has the cocktail made by bartender Don Carlos Orozco at Hussong's Cantina, in Ensenada, Mexico, named after his girlfriend. Yet another story takes place on July 4, 1942 in Juárez, Mexico, where according to Francisco "Pancho" Morales, a bartender in Tommy's Place, a favorite hangout for GI's from Fort Bliss, he concocted the cocktail. According to

Pancho, a woman entered the premises and ordered a cocktail called a *Magnolia*. He didn't know the ingredients so he whipped together his own version of a magnolia and called it a margarita—Spanish for daisy. Still another version (considered the most plausible) has the Margarita created in 1948 in Acapulco, Mexico, by a San Antonio, Texas socialite Margarita Sames. In an attempt to impress Nicky Hilton of the Hilton Hotel family, she mixed together three parts Tequila, two parts Cointreau, and one part lime juice.

Mary Pickford
A cocktail created in the 1920s, by Fred Kaufman, at the Hotel Nacional de Cuba, Havana. It was named in honor of Mary Pickford, wife of Douglas Fairbanks and popular star of silent films. At the time, she was in Cuba with her husband, and Charlie Chaplin, filming a movie. The petite blonde star was also known as "America's Sweetheart" and "Little Mary." The cocktail consists of rum, pineapple juice, and grenadine.

Martini
A cocktail consisting of gin or vodka and white dry vermouth, garnished with a lemon peel or green cocktail olive.

The martini, like many other cocktails' origins, is shrouded in mystery. One theory suggests that *Martinez* was the original name of this popular drink, first introduced in 1860 by Jerry Thomas in San Francisco's

Occidental Hotel. It was named after nearby Martinez, a local tourist stop for travelers. The local citizens there were so convinced that their town was the birthplace of the Martini that they installed a brass plaque to lay claim to that fact. The plaque reads in part, "On this site in 1874, Julio Richelieu, bartender, served up the first martini when a miner came into his saloon with a fistful of nuggets and asked for something special. He was served a Martinez Special." The original recipe was considerably different from what we now know. It consisted of one jigger of Old Tom Gin, one wine glass of sweet red vermouth, a dash of bitters, two dashes maraschino liqueur. It was then shaken well and garnished with lemon slice. That theory is also somewhat shaky because the first mention of the Martinez cocktail was in an 1884 bar book by O. H. Byron, and not Jerry Thomas. However, the first recorded mention of the Martini was in a bartender's guide published in the United States in 1888 and the drink was featured in an 1894 advertisement for a line of premixed cocktails. Another version states that a Signor Martini, a bartender at the Knickerbocker Hotel in New York, invented the Martini in the 1860s. At the same Knickerbocker Hotel in Manhattan, around 1912, bartender, Martini di Arma di Taggia, supposedly created the cocktail by mixing together equal parts of gin and dry (white) vermouth.

Other origins of the *martini cocktail* include the Italian version, which assumes the name comes from Martini & Rossi Vermouth, an indisputable ingredient. The British claim that the name originates with the Martini & Henry rifle (used between 1871 and 1891), known for its strong kick. The drink was really popularized by James Bond movies in which the super spy requested his vodka martini be served to him *shaken, not stirred.*

Milk Punch

A cocktail dating back to the late 1600s, consisting of milk, sugar, brandy, and rum. It has some similarities to egg nog.

Mojito

A cocktail consisting of white rum, sugar, lime juice, mint, and sparkling soda water. Regarding its origin, one popular story traces the cocktail to a similar sixteenth century cocktail called "El Draque" supposedly named after Sir Francis Drake and his pirates, who in 1586, tried to sack Havana, Cuba for its gold.

Monkey Gland

A cocktail consisting of gin, orange juice, grenadine, and anisette. It was popularized in the 1920s, by Dr. Serge Voronoff (1866–1951), a Russian refuge who migrated to France to perform experimental surgery. While at the Laboratory of Physiology in the College of France, he promoted the benefits of transplanting the sex glands of monkeys into human beings in order to restore vitality, prolong life, and sexual prowess. Years later, his theories were disproved and eventually dismissed.

Moscow Mule

A cocktail created and popularized in 1946 at the Cock N' Bull Restaurant in Los Angeles, California, by Jack Morgan (owner) and John Martin, president of Heublein, a spirits importer/distributor, while then trying to promote Smirnoff Vodka. It consists of vodka and ginger beer, with a wedge of lime.

Negroni

A cocktail consisting of Campari, gin, and sweet red vermouth, with a splash of seltzer and twist of lemon. Purportedly conceived around 1920 by a pub-crawling Count Camillo Negroni, of Florence, who demanded that Fosco Scarselli, the bartender at the Casoni bar in the Via Tornabuoni, add a shot of gin into his usual Americano cocktail.

Orange Blossom

A cocktail that is the same as a screwdriver, except that gin is substituted for the vodka. The drink was created during Prohibition as a way to cut the foul taste of illicitly produced gin.

Piña Colada

A cocktail consisting of rum, pineapple juice, and coconut milk. Purportedly concocted in 1963 by Don Ramos Portas Mingot, a bartender at the Barrachina Restaurant in San Juan, Puerto Rico. However, one

Ramón "Monchito" Marrero of Monchito's Bar at the Caribe Hilton in San Juan, Puerto Rico, claims he created it in 1952. Still another story has Don Ramón Lopez-Irizarry creating the drink the Puerto Rico in the 1960s.

Pink Gin

A cocktail from the mid-nineteenth century, made from gin mixed with a couple of dashes of Angostura bitters, which give it a pinkish color. It was given to British colonials and *Royal Navy* who consumed bitters as a preventive medicine. The cocktail was nicknamed, *Pinkers* by the Royal Navy. The Royal Navy is said to have favored Plymouth gin over London dry as the base gin, since it is fuller in flavor.

Pink Lady

A cocktail consisting of gin, applejack, lemon juice, grenadine, and an egg white; named after a play in 1911 of the same name and starring Hazel Dawn. In 1944, the Pink Lady enjoyed a revival in the play *Happy Birthday* in which Helen Hayes danced on the bar top after several drinks, including the Pink Lady.

Planter's Punch

A cocktail originally consisting of just rum, lime juice, sugar and water. The modern version from the 1940s consists of rum, pineapple juice, orange juice, lime juice, and grenadine syrup. It was supposedly made on the island of Jamaica in the late 1870s and not at the

Planter's Hotel in Charleston, South Carolina as some suggest.

Ramos Gin Fizz

A cocktail consisting of gin, lemon juice, lime juice, sugar, egg white, cream, and soda water; invented by Henry Charles Ramos in 1888, at his bar in Meyer's Restaurant in New Orleans. He later took it with him to the famous Imperial Cabinet Bar and Saloon in New Orleans.

Rompope

A type of eggnog consisting of eggs, rum, vanilla, sugar and almonds. The drink was created at the Convent of Santa Clara in Puebla, Mexico back in the early 1600s.

Rum & Coca-Cola

A cocktail consisting of rum and Coca-Cola with a twist of lime. The Andrew Sisters, a world-famous female singing group, began singing the song "Rum & Coca-Cola" to a war-torn Europe and America in 1944.

Rumrousal

A most unusual milk punch originating in New England consisting of Jamaican rum, whole milk, honey, and bourbon. The origin of this drink is unknown.

Ryumochki (*Russia*)

Small shot glasses (sometimes metal) used for drinking vodka straight.

Ryyppy (*Finland*)
A shot of ice-cold aquavit, schnapps, or vodka.

Salty Dog
A cocktail supposedly originating in the 1930s, consisting of gin and grapefruit juice, served in salted rim glass.

Samogon (*Russia*)
A bootlegged distilled spirit (moonshine) similar to vodka.

Sangrita
(Translates "little blood") A spicy nonalcoholic beverage generally drunk as a *chaser* after consuming tequila straight. It is a mixture of orange juice, lime juice, pomegranate juice, and hot chili sauce, giving it a *red* color. A more modern version calls for the addition of tomato juice, again for its red color. The drink was invented in the 1920s by Maria Guadalupe Nuño de Sánchez and her husband, José Edmundo at their Jalisco restaurant, La Viuda, in Mexico.

Screaming Orgasm
A cocktail consisting of Bailey's Irish Cream, Kahlúa, vodka, and cream.

Screwdriver
A cocktail consisting of vodka (or gin) and orange juice. This very popular drink was supposedly created in the

1950s, by American oil riggers stationed in the Middle East, who would use their screwdrivers to open cans of orange juice, then stir the vodka-orange juice mixture.

Sea Breeze

A cocktail developed in the 1960s, consisting of vodka, grapefruit juice, and cranberry juice.

Sex on the Beach

A cocktail consisting of vodka, peach schnapps, raspberry-flavored liqueur, pineapple juice, cranberry juice and an orange slice.

Shrub

A fruit drink made from citrus juice, rum, herbs, spices, and sugar; it was quite popular in eighteenth century England.

Silver Bullet

The name given to an extremely ice-cold, dry vodka martini during the 1950s and 1960s.

Singapore Gin Sling

A cocktail consisting of gin, cherry-flavored brandy, lemon and orange juice, and seltzer. Ngiam Tong Boon, a bartender at the Long Bar in the Raffles Hotel in Singapore, created this drink, originally called a *Straits Sling*, in 1915.

Sling
A cocktail from the early 1800s, in which a mug is filled two-thirds with strong beer and sweetened with sugar, molasses, or dried pumpkin. Rum is then added to this mixture and stirred with a loggerhead. It also is the name of a family of cocktails, often with gin as its base.

Sloe and Comfortable Screw
A cocktail consisting of vodka, Southern Comfort, sloe gin, and orange juice.

Southside
A cocktail consisting of gin, lemon juice, mint, and sugar syrup. The drink may have originated during Prohibition in Chicago, although the 21 Club in Manhattan claims the cocktail was first created at its establishment.

Stone Fence
A cocktail consisting of apple cider (or applejack), mixed with whiskey or even rum. This was popular in the late 1700s and was reputedly the favorite drink of Ethan Allen and his Green Mountain Boys. Stone Fence is also known as *stonewall* (United States).

Switchel
A colonial drink (originating in the Caribbean) consisting of rum, molasses, vinegar, ground ginger, and cold water.

Tequila Sunrise
A cocktail consisting of tequila, orange juice, and grenadine syrup. It was purportedly concocted in 1929, as a dawn pick-me-up at the American-financed gambling and gold resort at Agua Caliente, outside of Tijuana. It is also the name a 1973 song written by Don Henley and Glenn Frey and recorded by the Eagles.

Tom & Jerry
A cocktail consisting of an egg yolk, an egg white, sugar, allspice, white rum, and milk. Supposedly, the Tom & Jerry was created in 1847, by Professor Jerry Thomas, who named the drink after two, small white mice he had, "Tom" and the other "Jerry."

Tom Collins
A cocktail consisting of gin, lemon juice, sugar, and soda water. John Collins, the headwaiter waiter at the Limmer's Hotel and Coffee House on Conduit Street in London created the drink in the mid-1800s. He originally made the cocktail with Old Tom Gin. *See* John Collins.

Topless Margarita
A Margarita without a salted rim.

White Lady
A cocktail consisting of gin, lemon juice, and Cointreau. It is believed to have been created by Harry MacElhone

in 1919 at Ciro's Club in London. He originally used crème de menthe but replaced it with gin at Harry's New York Bar in Paris, in 1929.

White Russian
A cocktail consisting of vodka, Kahlúa, and cream.

Yale Cocktail
A cocktail consisting of gin, dry vermouth, blue curaçao, and orange bitters (the original recipe contained dry vermouth, gin, and crème d'Yvette). It was named after Yale University in New Haven, Connecticut, and although its origins are unknown, the cocktail was probably first concocted in the 1890s.

Zombie
A cocktail consisting of light rum, dark rum, gold rum, pineapple juice, papaya juice, lime juice, falernum or simple sugar, apricot-flavored brandy, orange curaçao or passion fruit syrup, and 151 proof Demerara rum. It was developed in 1934, by Los Angeles restaurateur Don the Beachcomber (Ernest Raymond Beaumont-Gantt) that featured perhaps every type of rum he had on hand at his bar. Supposedly, he concocted it for a friend who had dropped by his restaurant before flying to San Francisco. The friend left after having consumed three of them. He returned several days later to say that he had been turned into a zombie for his entire trip.

Yet, another version states Don concocted it to help a hung-over customer get through a business meeting. He returned several days later to complain that he too, had been turned into a zombie for his entire trip. This drink boasted an infamous campaign that many simply could not pass up: "O*nly one to a customer.*"

"Of all the gin joints in all the towns in all the world, she walks into mine." (Humphrey Bogart, 1899–1957, American film actor; as Rick Blaine in *Casablanca*, 1942)

GENERAL INFORMATION ABOUT
DISTILLED SPIRITS

"America's lethal weapon." (Nikita Khrushchev, 1894–1971, *First Secretary of the Central Committee of the Communist Party of the Soviet Union*)

What is the shelf life of an opened bottle of distilled spirits and does it need any special storage conditions? A bottle of distilled spirits has an extremely long shelf life due to its high alcohol level (generally 40 percent, alcohol-by-volume or 80 proof). It will last almost indefinitely opened or unopened, unless subjected to extremely hot or cold temperatures for prolonged periods of time. Distilled spirits react quite well to direct sunlight.

Can bottles of Vodka, Gin, Rum, or Tequila be safely stored in the freezer?

Yes. They won't freeze because of their high alcohol content. They may however, become somewhat thick and almost syrupy.

How do some Rum and Tequila obtain their brown color?

Spirits typically obtains its characteristic brown color from any of these four sources: coloring matter from the barrel, oxidation, charred barrels (also the "red" inner layer), and the addition of caramel for color adjustment.

Can the quality of Rum or Tequila be determined by its color?

No. Some spirits are lightly tinted with amber or brown color, while others certainly have much more of a richer, mahogany color. The addition of caramel for color adjustment is just one of many tools the master distiller has to be certain the spirit just-being-bottled looks identical to the one bottled last year, and (hopefully) next year. Distillers also have a "house color," which they try to emulate with each bottling. ("House color" is a color preference for their spirit, which is maintained batch-to-batch and year-after-year and never changes.) Therefore, if you conduct a rum or tequila tasting, don't expect the ones containing more color to be fuller-bodied; it's just not true.

Do Vodka, Gin, Rum, or Tequila age or improve after being bottled?

No: aging **only** takes place in wooden barrels; when removed, the product ceases to age **or** improve. While in the barrel, complex changes take place. Aging smoothes a rough, new spirit and adds bouquet and character. The process of mellowing an alcoholic beverage is through extraction, as the alcohol dissolves flavor-affecting chemicals present in the wood of the barrels. Flavor components, aromatic substances, and wood tannin all contribute to the body, character, and complexity of the distilled spirit.

During aging, the liquid nearest the barrel wall becomes denser from taking on the added weight of the extractables; this heavier liquid then falls away, causing circulation, which brings the lighter liquid from the center of the barrel to the walls to pick up added extractable elements. The smaller the barrel, the more rapid the circulation and the extraction, and hence the more rapid the aging process.

Therefore, a bottle of 15-year old rum, which was purchased 10 years ago, is still 15-years old (although you are now 10 years older!)

What is Turbinado Sugar?

A partially refined, coarse-grained, beige-colored crystal containing the molasses portion of the sugar. Those crystals are then spun in a centrifuge or turbine, to separate any remaining juice from the crystals— these turbines give *turbinado* its name. It is occasionally used in rum production. *See* Demerara Rum.

101 THINGS YOU NEED TO KNOW

ABOUT VODKA, GIN, RUM, & TEQUILA

I n this section, I discuss "101 Things You Need To Know About Vodka, Gin, Rum, and Tequila" sometimes as a question and other times as a statement of fact. See how many you know and enjoy reading the rest of the book with a glass of spirits. Cheers!

distilled from a type agave

Types of "Clear Spirits"

Dutch gin
Bols, Bom's a like gin

The major categories of clear spirits are covered, which include Vodka, Gin, Rum, and Tequila along with other similar product such as Aquavit, Cachaça, Genever, Mezcal, Schnapps, and still others.

Scandinavian liquor of caraway seeds

distilled fruit brandies, herbal, infusions or adding fruit juice, artificial flavoring. Base is neutral grain spirits

Brazilian liq distilled from sugar cane

56

Vodka (Aquavit, Schnapps)

"A martini, Shaken, not stirred." (James Bond "Sean Connery" *Goldfinger*, 1964)

1. What exactly is Vodka?

An alcoholic distillate from a fermented mash of primarily grain; it is distilled at or above 190 proof, bottled at not less than 80 proof (except in the case of flavored vodkas), and processed further to extract all congeners with the use of activated charcoal. According to the United States federal standards of identity, U.S.-made vodka must be "without distinctive character, aroma, taste, or color." However, no federal regulations require vodka to be entirely without aroma or taste; therefore, some vodkas display distinctive characteristics in aroma and taste.

2. What's the origin of Vodka?

Vodka seems to have first appeared in either Russia or Poland around the twelfth century, when it was known as *zhizenennia voda* (water of life) in the Russian monastery-fort of Viatka. The word *vodka* comes from the Russian word for water, *voda* or the Polish word *wódka* (in Polish the *w* has a *v* sound). The suffix "*ka*" was added to the root word centuries later. By the fourteenth century, vodka began to be used as a beverage; formerly, it was mainly used in perfumes and cosmetics. However, it was primarily employed as the base ingredient of many wonder drugs or cure-all elixirs. During the fifteenth century, Poland produced many types of vodka as well as several "grades," which varied according to the number of times the vodka was distilled and refined. Until the sixteenth century, vodka was known in Poland as *gorzale wino* or *gorzalka*, which meant "scorched" or "distilled wine," in order to distinguish it from beverages made from medicinal vodkas. At that time, rye was the chief ingredient in most vodka production. Also in the fifteenth century, Swedish distillers began using locally grown wheat to produce a form of neutral spirits they referred to as "brännvin" or *burnt wine*. This brännvin was originally used for medicinal purposes—but later on, because of the pleasing effects, gained popularity for general consumption.

In the sixteenth and seventeenth centuries, vodka consumption grew dramatically. Vodka became the national drink of Russia, Poland, and Sweden.

3. What are some of the countries where Vodka is made?

Vodka is produced in Austria, Australia, Belgium, Canada, China, Czech Republic, Denmark, England, Estonia, Finland, France, Georgia, Germany, Greenland, Iceland, India, Ireland, Israel, Italy, Japan, Latvia, Lithuania, Mexico, Netherlands, New Zealand, Norway,

Poland, Russia, Scotland, Slovakia, Spain, Sweden, Switzerland, Turkey, Ukraine, and the United States, among others.

4. What is Vodka made from?

Grains—(barley, corn, rice, rye, wheat), sugar beets, grapes, maple syrup, molasses, plums, potatoes, sugarcane. Actually, vodka can be made from virtually any ingredient that contains starch or sugar.

Vodka was originally made from the most plentiful and least expensive ingredients available, which in most cases was rye or the potato. Its popularity soared in the 1820s due to more abundant and better potato crops. The potato is assumed to be a cheap and plentiful ingredient. In fact, only special varieties of potatoes (generally *Stobrawa, Glada, Mila,* and *Solist,* to name but a few) with a starch content of about 22 percent (generally twice that of boiling potatoes) are used. These potatoes are actually more expensive to harvest and prepare for distillation than grain. It is estimated that it takes about ten pounds of potatoes to produce one liter of vodka. Using potatoes as a base is the most complicated due to the difficulty breaking down the starches and converting to fermentable sugars. Potato mash produces more flavorful and heavier vodka. However, nowadays, grain rules as the main base ingredient for vodka throughout the world. The early vodkas, even if made from grains, were strongly flavored, and therefore it became a common practice to add herbs, spices, and fruits to mask the sometimes harsh, raw taste of the grain. In 1564, King Jan Olbracht passed a law that allowed every citizen to make vodka at home. These vodkas were made and usually flavored with whatever ingredients were in abundance. In 1870, the Russian Tsar hired a chemist, Theodore Lowitz to produce vodka more hygienically. He invented a technique for purifying vodka by filtration though charcoal.

5. Is Vodka aged, like whiskey?
Most vodka is not aged and federal regulations do not permit age claims, distillation date, or vintage date. Vodka may be stored in containers of stainless steel, porcelain, concrete, glass, paraffin, or any other neutral material—rarely wood. Vodka does not need aging due to the neutrality of the spirit (190 proof or higher) and filtering through charcoal, which renders it virtually free of *congeners* that would otherwise need barrel aging to soften.

- **Congeners**: Trace-flavoring constituents vaporized off with the alcohol in distillation above 190 proof and developed and expanded during the aging process. Congeners, which are produced during the fermenting process, are made up of fusel oils, esters, tannins, acids, aldehydes, as well as others. In proper proportion with other elements, these components contribute to palatability and create the characteristic aroma, body, and taste of a particular distilled spirit. When the spirit is distilled at a lower proof, more congeners are present and the spirit will possess more character.

6. What are the classifications of Vodka?

There are no world-wide uniform classifications or standards for vodka. In the EU, vodka must have a minimum alcohol of 37.5 percent. If the vodka is not made from potatoes or grain, an EU producer must state the products used in fermentation on the label.

Poland grades vodka according to their degree of purity: standard (zwykly), premium (wyborowy) and deluxe (luksusowy). In Russia, vodka that is labeled osobaya (special) usually is a superior-quality product, while krepkaya (strong) denotes an overproof vodka of at least 56% alcohol (112 proof).

7. What are the types of Vodka produced?

There two types—unflavored and flavored (American and imported)

8. What is Flavored Vodka?

According to U.S. federal regulations (1992), flavored vodkas are a mixture of distilled spirits that are flavored and colored with various types of fruit and/or herbs and may or may not contain added sugar. Some flavors are apple, bacon, berry, birch, black cherry, black truffle, blood orange, blueberry, caramel, celery, cherry, chocolate, cilantro, cinnamon, citrus, coconut, cola, cranberry, cucumber, currant, dill, espresso, fennel, garlic, ginger, grapefruit, green tea, green walnuts, honey, lavender, lemon, lime, mango, melon, mint, orange, peach, pear, pepper (hot), pineapple, plum, pomegranate, raspberry, rosemary, rowanberry, strawberry, tomato, vanilla, and watermelon, plus many others. They are bottled at not less than 60 proof (30 percent alcohol by volume) and the name of the predominant flavor *must* appear on the label.

9. What are some examples of "specialty flavored" Vodka from Poland, Russia, and other Slavic Countries?

Chesnochnaya (*Poland or Russia*) Vodka infused with a combination of garlic, pepper, and dill.

Cytrynówka (*Poland*) Vodka flavored with the aromatics of fresh lemon peels and lemon leaves.

Mysliwska (*Poland*) A hunter's vodka flavored with juniper berries and herbs. (The term *hunter's vodka* originates from the tradition in which the aristocrats of Czarist Russia drank such vodkas to celebrate a successful hunt.)

Pieprzówka (*Poland*) Vodka flavored with Turkish black pepper and paprika.

Sliwowica (*Poland*) Vodka flavored with ripe plums and generally aged in oak barrels for several years.

Starka (*Poland* and *Russia*) An amber-colored vodka dating back to the sixteenth century. It is one of the few available aged vodkas (up to ten years) and is flavored with brandy, port (or Malaga), honey, and vanilla, plus the leaves of several different types of Crimean apple and pear trees. Starka can also be produced from 100 percent rye grain. Starka is also produced in other Slavic countries.

Zubrówka (*Poland* and *other Slavic Countries*) A flavored vodka produced since at least the sixteenth century. It has a yellow-green tinge and a distinctive smell and taste of spring flowers, thyme, lavender, and freshly mown grass, which is derived from various botanicals that have been added. Bottles contain a single blade of *Hierochloe odorata* grass from the Bialowieza Forest, a National Park in Eastern Poland. In 1978, United States scientists believed that the grass contained *coumarin*, a toxic compound found in some plants, believed to thin blood and possibly cause liver cancer. The vodka was pulled from the United States, but since has returned and is free from any harmful substances. It is also known in the United States as *Bison Vodka* or *Buffalo Vodka* and in Russia, it is spelled *Zubrovka*.

Zytnia (*Poland*) Vodka made from rye with aromatic hints of fruit (apple, pear). The name supposedly comes from the word used to describe the smile of a village elder or mayor.

10. When did imported Vodka enter the United States?

Peter (Pyotr) Smirnoff first began making vodka in Moscow in 1818 (actually, the Smirnoff family was not Russian; they came from Lvov, Poland). Immediately after World War I (1917), the Bolsheviks gained control of Russia and Vladimir Smirnoff (descendant of Peter) was forced into exile in Paris.

It wasn't until 1934 that Rudolph Kunett (Kunnetchansky) first introduced vodka commercially into the United States. He was of Ukrainian extraction and his father sold grain and alcohol to the Cast Iron Bridge Distillery of Moscow. Kunett bought the American rights to Smirnoff from Vladimir Smirnoff for the sum of $2,500.00. Kunett originally set up business in Bethel, Connecticut with the American branch of Societe Pierre (Peter) Smirnoff et Fils, but the venture did not prosper. He then met John G. Martin, the English-born president of the small but long-respected Hartford-based firm of Heublein. Against strong opposition, Martin arranged to retain Kunett and in 1939

Heublein purchased the Smirnoff name and formula for a mere $14,000 (plus some royalties), taking over its production and sales. For many years, Smirnoff vodka used the slogan, "It will leave you breathless." During the 1950s and 1960s, Smirnoff called their ice-cold, dry vodka martini "The Silver Bullet."

11. Many people when ordering a Vodka Martini ask that no vermouth be added. Is this a Martini?

No. It is Vodka on-the-rocks and nothing more. Vermouth, along with vodka or gin is what makes a martini, a "Martini!"

12. Should bottles of premium Vodka should be stored in the freezer?

They can be. Vodka won't freeze because of the high alcohol level and it will be instantly at the right temperature for mixing your favorite cocktail without melting the ice cubes. Vodka is often enjoyed Arctic cold, served in *Y-shaped* glasses or *ryumochki* (small shot glasses) and downed in one gulp.

13. Some Brands of Vodka
American-Made:

3-Vodka, Argent, Aristocrat, Bellow's, Bocaj, Burnett's, Charbay, Crown Russe, Crystal Palace, Deep Eddy, Duggan's, Flying Point. Gilbey's, Gordon's, Herb's Aromatic, Kamchatka, Liquid Ice, New Amsterdam,

Nikolai, Platinum 7X, Popov, Prairie, Rain, Roth, Seagram's, Skol, Skyy, Smirnoff, Taaka Platinum 7X, Tito's, Tvarscki, UV, Wolfschmidt, Zemkoff

Imported:
(Austria): Monopolowa; (Canada): Pearl, Silhouette; (China): Great Wall, Tsing Tao; (Czech Republic): Jelinek Bohemia Plum; (Denmark): Danzka, Denaka, Frïs, Karlsson's Gold; (England): Borzoi, Burrough's, Tanqueray Sterling; (Estonia): Türi; (Finland): Finlandia; (France): Alps, Cîroc, Citadelle, Gold Flakes Supreme, Grey Goose, Ice Diamonds, Jean Marc XO, Vertical, X-Rated; (Greenland): Sermeq; (Iceland): Elduris, Icy; (Ireland): Boru; (Israel): Carmel; (Italy): Mezzaluna, Roberto Cavalli; (Japan): Suntory; (Moldova): Exclusiv; (Netherlands): Blavod, Bong, Ketel One, P.I.N.K., V2, Vincent Van Gogh, Vox; (Norway): Vikingfjord; (Poland): Baks Boonekamp, Belvedere, Chopin, Królewska, Luksusowa, Ultimat, Wyborowa, Zubrówka; (Russia): Cristall, Kremlyovskaya, Kutskova, Moryoskoff, Moskovskaya, Priviet, Royal Dragon, Ruskova, Staraya Moskva, Stolichnaya, Zyr; (Sweden): Absolut, Camitz Svedka; (Turkey): Izmira; (Ukraine): Goldenbarr

14. Popular Cocktails
Black Russian, Bloody Mary, Blue Lagoon, Bullshot, Bullshot, Cape Codder, Cosmopolitan, Gibson, Godmother, Harvey Wallbanger, Kamikaze, Martini, Moscow Mule,

Screaming Orgasm, Screwdriver, Sea Breeze, Sex on the Beach, Silver Bullet, Sloe and Comfortable Screw, White Russian

15. What is Aquavit?

The national beverage of Scandinavian (*Denmark, Finland, Iceland, Norway,* and *Sweden*) countries, is a high proof spirit, which literally means "water of life." The first Swedish license to sell aquavit was granted in Stockholm in 1498, and in 1555, King Christian III of Denmark established a royal distillery for the brewing of aquavit.

16. What is Aquavit made from?

It is made from a distillate of grain or potatoes (neutral spirits) and redistilled (at a lower proof due to the addition of water) in the presence of caraway seeds, fruits, herbs, and spices, which may include anise, cardamom, cinnamon, coriander, cumin, dill, fennel, and ginger. The final product has the neutrality of vodka with a pronounced caraway flavor. Because of its potency, it was nicknamed "Black Death." Aquavit is not ordinarily aged, but when it is, the spirit takes on a brownish color.

17. Which spelling is correct: Aquavit or Akvavit?

In Denmark, it is spelled *akvavit* and often known as *snaps*, and in Norway it is spelled *aquavit*. Aquavit is also known as *brännvin* "burned wine."

18. How is Aquavit served traditionally?

It is generally served icy–cold, although it can be sipped neat in small glasses. It is often served with beer or followed by a beer "chaser" as an accompaniment to salty, spicy, or pungent foods such as anchovies, herring, kippers, and lox. It is also the essential companion to pork and other high fat meats; but it also goes well with crabs, prawns, mussels, and fish.

19. Are there any cocktails using Aquavit?

Glögg, is a traditional hot-spiced drink of Sweden, similar to hot mulled wine, usually consumed during the cold weather. It is made from a combination of aquavit or brandy, wine, cardamom seeds, cloves, sugar, raisins, almonds, and other ingredients. Glögg is served warm in glasses containing a small cinnamon stick, raisins, currants, or almonds.

20. Some Brands of Aquavit

Aalborg (Denmark); Explorer (Sweden); Linie (Norway); O.P. Anderson (Sweden); Renat (Sweden)

21. What is Schnapps?

Schnapps is a northern European (*Germany, Netherlands,* and *Scandinavia*) generic term for a high-proof alcoholic beverage, especially the clear, unaged distilled spirits such as vodka, gin, and akvavit. A clear, white distilled spirit whose distinctive aroma or taste (similar to vodka), made from grain, potatoes, fruits, or herbs, which is often flavored with numerous aromatic herbs. Usually consumed neat and often flavored with fruit essences or caraway seeds. (It should not be confused with American-made schnapps, which is a liqueur.) Schnapps is also spelled *snaps.*

"Before I start to write, I always treat myself to a nice dry martini. Just one, to give me the courage to get started. After that, I am on my own." (Elwyn Brooks "E. B." White, 1899–1985, American writer, *New Yorker Magazine*)

Gin (Genever)

"Last night I had *tee many martoonies!*" (Dean Martin, 1917–1995, American singer and actor)

22. What exactly is Gin?

According to the United States Standards of Identity, gin is an alcoholic distillate, colorless to pale yellow in color, from a fermented mash of primarily grain; it is distilled at or above 190 proof, bottled at not less than 80 proof (except in the case of flavored gins), and processed further to extract all congeners with the use of activated charcoal. Under U.S. federal regulations, gin can be made either by direct distillation (or redistillation) or the compound method. Distilled gins are allowed to use the word *distilled* on the label, although gins made through the *compound method* are not. According to 2008 *EU* regulations, compound gin may be labeled *gin*, but not "distilled or "London Gin." London Dry Gin cannot be colored.

23. What are some of the countries where Gin is made?

Gin is made in many countries including Australia, Belgium, Canada, England, France, Germany, Hungary, Ireland, Netherlands, New Zealand, Philippines, Poland, Scotland, Spain, Sweden, and the United States.

24. What is the History & Background of Gin?

Genever (Gin) was being distilled in the mid-1500s, although records don't exist as to the precise date of distillation. In 1585, Queen Elizabeth I of England, sent Robert Dudley, Earl of Leicester to help the Dutch gain independence from Spain during the Eighty Years War (1568–1648). Supposedly, the British soldiers noticed the "local soldiers" drinking a shot of "genever" before battle to give them "courage;" from which the term, *Dutch Courage* is believed to have originated. The British soldiers sampled the juniper-flavored distilled spirit and found it to their liking and returning home in 1587, they shared tales of victory and spread word of what they'd begun to refer to as "Dutch courage." They also brought along with the name *genever*, mistakenly thought to be a product from Switzerland. The name was changed to *gen*, which was later Anglicized to *gin*. In no time at all gin became the national drink of England, which continues to this day.

Some research claims that Genever (or some other juniper-infused spirit) was made in Salerno, Italy in the eleventh century due to the abundance of juniper berries. Another story states that in the late 1400s, the Dutch were distilling large quantities of spirits from cereals, mainly rye. Still another source states that the first English Gin was made in 1485, in the court of King Henry VII. Most books and articles erroneously give credit for creating gin to Franz de la Boë (1614–1672) whose Latin name was Franciscus Sylvius. Dr. Sylvius was a physician and professor of medicine at Holland's famed University of Leiden and supposedly invented genever (gin) in 1650.

25. What was the Gin Act?

In 1736 Parliament passed the Gin Act which imposed a prohibitive duty per gallon on the retailer and raised the cost of a distilling license. This act was due to pressure by politicians and religious leaders who claimed that gin drinking encouraged laziness, public drunkenness and other criminal behavior. However, gin continued to be distilled in homes as well as by large distillers and the law was circumvented by calling their product "Parliamentary Brandy" or any other term, except for Gin. The Gin Act was repealed in 1743 and replaced in 1751 by a more equitable tax structure.

26. What is Gin made from?

The important differences among gins are the result of the type of mash from which the neutral spirits are distilled, the quality of the juniper berries, and other botanicals used in the redistillation process. The flavoring content of the botanicals used changes from year to year, depending on rainfall, amount of sunshine received, and so on, so the distiller must alter his formula every year in order to achieve the same taste and smell, bottle after bottle.

According to U.S. federal regulations and *EU* regulations, gin must derive its predominant flavor from juniper berries. U.S. federal regulations "Standards of Identity" permit gin to be produced from any of the following base materials: barley, corn, rye, wheat, sugarcane, and other agricultural products. Most gins are produced by private formulas, which are the distillers' most closely guarded secret. Known ingredients or botanicals besides juniper berries that are often used in small proportions are: angelica root, anise, bitter almonds, calamus, caraway seeds, cardamom, cassia bark, cinnamon, cocoa nibs, coriander seeds, cubeb berries, cumin, dragon eye, fennel, ginger, grains of paradise, lemons or dried lemon peel, lavender, licorice, limes, lotus leaves, nutmeg, orange peel, orris root, poppy, savory, spruce, tangerine, violet root, and other seeds, and almost a limitless number of barks, herbs, and roots.

27. What are Juniper Berries?

An aromatic berry of an evergreen shrub, which is round and dark purplish blue. The finest berries usually come from Italy, Albania, Croatia, and Serbia. They are spicy with a bitter-sweet taste and overtones of pine, lavender, banana, and camphor. The oils from the berries are used in the making of gin and some liqueurs. Juniper berries are known as *genièvre* (France) and *ginepro* (Italy).

28. Production Methods for Gin

After the initial distillation, the producer uses many different methods to produce the characteristic juniper aroma and flavor. U.S. federal regulations acknowledge the existence of different styles of gin; however, it only defines two types. They are *distilled* gin and *compound* gin. After distillation, the proof of the gin is corrected with distilled water and then bottled.

Distilled Gin: An alcoholic beverage obtained from the original distillate of mash or by the redistillation of distilled spirits with juniper berries and other aromatics customarily used in making gin. The method is to suspend the cracked and crushed juniper berries on mesh trays, baskets, or perforated racks called *gin heads*. This allows rising vapors to pass from the still through and around the berries, allows them to pick up essences and become impregnated with the aromatic flavoring oils of the botanicals, which remain in the condensed distillate. These accumulated vapors are then condensed and used in making gin.

Compound Gin: Gin produced by mixing or soaking high-proof neutral distilled spirits with extracts or oils of the juniper berry and other botanicals and flavorings. This gin is of a lower quality than distilled gin, therefore very little is produced using this method. This is, however, a federally approved definition that recalls the days of Prohibition, when members of households mixed neutral distilled spirits (often using methyl alcohol or wood alcohol, which is lethal, instead of ethyl alcohol) with juniper or *gin flavoring* to produce a bootleg distilled spirit called *bathtub gin* or *hooch*. Distilled gins are allowed to use the word *distilled* on the label, although gins made through the *compound method* are not. According to 2008 *EU* regulations, compound gin may be labeled *gin*, but not "distilled or "London Gin."

29. Is Gin aged, like whiskey?
Most gin is not aged and federal regulations do not permit age claims, distillation date, or vintage date. Gin may be stored in containers of stainless steel, porcelain, concrete, glass, paraffin, or any other neutral material—rarely wood. Gin does not need aging due to the neutrality of the spirit (190 proof or higher) and filtering through charcoal, which renders it virtually free of congeners that would otherwise need barrel aging to soften.

What are some types of Gin produced?

30. American Dry Gin.
American gins are usually produced by one of two methods, *distilling* or *compounding*. They are often labeled *dry* or *extra dry*, although these terms have little actual meaning and gins labeled as such are not actually any drier than other gins. American dry gins are ideal for use in cocktails. In the 1870s, Fleischmann's produced the first American dry gin in the United States.

31. London Dry Gin
A generic name for gin lacking sweetness. In England, gin mash usually contains less corn and more barley, because English distillers believe this produces a distilled

spirit of extraordinary smoothness. Their gins are distilled at a high proof and then redistilled in the presence of juniper berries. London gins have a lightly balanced, aromatic juniper bouquet and flavor; they are light, dry, crisp, and clean, with the delicate flavoring of the juniper berry, although this is slightly toned down. London dry gin cannot be colored. London dry gins, although originally produced only in or near London in the early 1830s, are now produced all over the world, with the term, considered generic, having little meaning. The first *dry* gin produced without heavy sugar syrup, was made in London in the early 1830s. London Dry Gin is also known as *British Gin, English Gin*, and *Dry Gin.*

32. Golden Gin
A gin (originally from England) aged in oak barrels for a short time and has a light golden-brown color, extracted from the barrel. Golden gin is quite difficult to find nowadays.

33. Gin Liqueur
A liqueur bottled at not less than 60 proof, in which the distilled spirit used is entirely gin, and that possesses a predominant characteristic gin flavor derived from the distilled spirit used.

34. Old Tom Gin
A pot stilled gin, usually sweetened (3 to 6 percent) by the addition of sugar syrup (sometimes orange flower

water), which was quite popular during the eighteenth century. The name supposedly comes from a colorful character named Captain Dudley Bradstreet, who is said to have nailed a sign in the shape of a cat to his London house and with a metal tube, which extended through the window, served gin through the cat's paw. Payment was through the cat's mouth. It is rarely seen nowadays. It was the original gin in the classic *Tom Collins* drink, while the John Collins was made with *genever* (gin). Gordon's made Old Tom Gin until the 1970s.

35. Plymouth Gin

This is actually an *appellation* for gin and is only produced by the Coates firm of Plymouth, England, which was founded in 1793. The distillery was actually named after the Dominican Order of Black Friars who erected a monastery on the site in 1431. Plymouth gin was originally associated with the British Royal Navy, which, as legend has it, invented this gin as a tolerable way of drinking bitters (quinine), which helped control intestinal disorders. They often mixed it with lime juice; hence the nickname *limey*, which is frequently applied to the British.

- An *appellation* is a legally defined and protected geographical indication used to identify where certain products are produced.

Plymouth Gin is an aromatic gin, made from juniper, lemon and orange peel, coriander, cardamom, angelica root and orris root, which makes it earthier and softer. Plymouth Gin is sometimes pink in color from the addition of Angostura bitters. Its taste lies somewhere between that of Dutch and London dry gin.

36. Steinhäger Gin
A gin produced in Westphalia, Germany, containing only juniper berries and no other botanicals. It is similar to London dry types, but with slightly less of a juniper smell and taste. Steinhäger is also spelled *Steinhäeger.*

37. What is Flavored Gin?
According to U.S. federal regulations (1992), flavored gins are a mixture of distilled spirits that are flavored and colored with various types of fruit and/or herbs and may or may not contain added sugar. Some flavors are apple, cherry, cranberry, cucumber, elderflower, grapefruit, lemon, lime, mint, orange, peach, pineapple, plum, raspberry, rhubarb, and saffron, plus others. They are bottled at not less than 60 proof (30 percent alcohol by volume) and the name of the predominant flavor *must* appear on the label.

38. I heard that gin could be called a *liqueur*, if it were sweetened. Is this true?
Yes it is true. The three elements for a beverage to be classified a liqueur are: a base of alcohol (Gin certain has that); flavoring (gin— juniper berries); minimum 2-1/2 percent sugar (No sugar in gin).

39. Is Sloe Gin a type of "Gin?"

No, it is not actually a gin, but rather a red liqueur made from *sloe* (little blackberries berries) that grows in bluish-black bunches on blackthorn trees, which gives it a rather tart plum flavor. Originally the sloe berries were soaked in gin, although some commercially made sloe gins use less expensive neutral grain spirits.

40. Which is drier, a Gin or Vodka Martini?

They are both equally dry. The confusion lies in the perfume of the juniper berry (and other botanicals) in gin, which is sometimes mistakenly confused with "sweetness."

41. Some Brands of Gin
American-Made:

Aviation, Barton, Bellows, Calvert, Chatham, Clyde's, Fleischmann's, Georgi, Gilbey's, Gordon's, Hiram Walker, Junipero, Old Mr. Boston, Seagram's, Stonecutter

Imported:

(Australia): Vicker's; (Canada): Ungava; (England): Bafferts, Beefeater, Boodles, Bombay, Boord's, Booth's, Bull Dog, Burnett's, Corney & Barrow, Daresbury's Quintessential, Hendrick's, Kensington, Martin Miller, Plymouth, Squires, Tanqueray, The London No. 1; (France): Citadelle, Magellan; (Germany): Doornkaat, Schlichte, Schinkenhaeger; (Netherlands): Bols, Fockink, Leyden, Vincent Van Gogh; (New Zealand): Lighthouse

42. What is a Pimm's Cup?

A "gin sling," flavored with various herbs, spices, and sweeteners, was invented in 1841, by James Pimm, proprietor of Pimm's Oyster Bar, London, England. Years back, Pimm's Cup was produced in six different versions, each with a different base ingredient, and identified by a number of the label. For instance: Pimm's Cup #1, 2, 3, 4, 5, 6. But because the gin version (No. 1) comprised 99 percent of total sales, the other variations were dropped in 1974. The base ingredients of Pimm's Cup are as follows: #1 Gin; #2 Whiskey; #3 Brandy; #4 Rum; #5 Rye Whiskey; #6 Vodka.

43. Popular Cocktails

Alabama Slammer, Bronx Cocktail, Christy Girl, Dog's Nose, Gibson, Gimlet, Gin and It, Gin Fizz, John Collins, Long Island Iced Tea, Martini, Monkey Gland, Negroni, Orange Blossom, Pink Gin, Pink Lady, Ramos Gin Fizz, Salty Dog, Singapore Gin Sling, Southside, Tom Collins, White Lady, Yale Cocktail

44. What is Genever?

A gin produced primarily in Holland from a low-proof, distilled malt spirit, which is re-distilled with juniper and other botanicals, resulting in a heavier body than the dry gins produced in the United States and England. Another general characteristic of genever is that it retains and imparts some of the taste and odor of the grains (rye, corn, and wheat). Genever takes its name from the juniper berries (*genever*) and is often sold in brown earthenware bottles known *cruchons*. Also spelled *jenever*. Genever is also known in the Netherlands as *Dutch Gin, Holland Gin,* and *Schiedam*.

45. How is Genever made?

The production of Dutch gin is slightly different from that of other gin; the Dutch usually begin with a grain mash of rye, corn, and wheat, distilled in a *pot still* at around 100 to 110 proof. The initial distillate, known as *moutwijn* (malt wine), is then redistilled in the presence of juniper berries in another *pot still*, which carries flavoring congeners and produces Dutch gin's full-bodied character. Dutch gins are usually heavy, with very complex, malty aromas and flavors; they have a pungent, full taste of juniper berries. They also have a pronounced grain flavor and, surprisingly, are occasionally slightly sweet. Due to their heaviness of taste, they are usually drunk straight and cold, especially in Holland.

46. What are some terms associated with Genever?

Cruchons: Brown earthenware bottles used to house Genever.

Jonge: Young; used when referring to Genever.

Korngenever: A Genever made solely from corn.

Moutwijn: "Malt Wine." A low-alcohol, distilled spirit utilized for Genever, which is rich in both texture and flavor. The greater percent of *moutwijn* in the blend, the fuller the body.

Oude: Old; used when referring to Genever.

Schiedam Gin: A gin named after a Dutch town (near Rotterdam) where it is distilled.

"I exercise extreme self-control I never drink anything stronger than gin before breakfast." (W. C. Fields, 1880–1946, American Comic and Actor)

Rum (Cachaça)

"Fifteen men on the Dead Man's Chest-
Yo-ho-ho, and a bottle of rum!
Drink and the devil had done for the rest-
Yo-ho-ho, and a bottle of rum!" (Robert Louis Stevenson, 1850–1894, Scottish Author and Critic, from *Treasure Island*)

47. What exactly is Rum?

Rum is an alcoholic distillate from the fermented juice of sugar cane, sugar cane syrup, sugar cane molasses, or other sugar cane by-products. It is produced at less than 190 proof in such manner that the distillate possesses the taste, aroma, and characteristics generally attributed to rum, and bottled at not less than 80 proof (except in the case of flavored rum) and also includes mixtures solely of such distillates. Some rums are bottled at 151-proof.

48. What is Molasses?

A thick, dark brown syrup that is generally sweet. It is the by-product of the manufacture of sugar from sugarcane in which the syrup is separated from the crystals using a centrifuge. The highest grade is *light* molasses (about 70 percent sugar), which has a mild flavor and sometimes used as table syrup. The lowest grade is *blackstrap molasses* (about 55 percent sugar), which is often used in the production of caramel and some dark rums.

The word blackstrap is derived from the Dutch *stroop*, for syrup.

49. What are some of the countries where Rum is made?

Rum is produced mainly in Caribbean, Central and South American countries—Anguilla, Antigua, Bahamas, Barbados, Bermuda, Brazil, Colombia, Costa Rica, Cuba, Dominican Republic, Ecuador, Grenada, Guadeloupe, Guatemala, Guyana, Haiti, Jamaica, Martinique, Mexico, Nicaragua, Panama, Puerto Rico, St. Croix, St. Lucia, Tobago, Trinidad, Venezuela, and the Virgin Islands. Rum is also produced in Australia, Austria, Canada, Czech Republic, Germany, Great Britain, Hawaii, India, Madagascar, Nepal, New Zealand, Philippines, South Africa, Spain, the United States, and other parts of the world. Rum is known as *rhum* (France) and *ron* (Spanish).

50. What is the History & Background of Rum?

No one knows for sure where the name rum comes from; some believe it is a shortened version of the word *Saccharum officinarum*, which is Latin for "sugarcane." However, others believe that the name came from the term *rumbullion*, a mid-1600s term for rum that originated in the West Indies.

In 1493, Columbus brought sugarcane to the West Indies from the Canary Islands on his second voyage. In the 1520s, Portuguese explorers soon began transporting sugarcane in much the same manner to Brazil. By the year 1600, rum production began on the island of Barbados and in 1651, rum was called *Barbados water, rumbullion,* or *kill-devil.*

The first distillery in what is now the United States was built in 1640, on Staten Island (New York City) by William Keift, Director-General of the New Netherlands. This facility was already producing rum when the English seized the Dutch colony in 1664. Another rum distillery was operating in Massachusetts as early as 1667. Rum, distilled in New England, was transported to Africa, perhaps with stops at Madeira, the Azores, or the Canaries, where some of it was sold. Rum was America's favorite drink long before bourbon was even invented. In 1775, more than 12 million gallons of rum were consumed annually in the 13 colonies, a significant amount for a population that was still under three million at the time. The early popularity of rum in this country lessened because of the Embargo Act of 1807, which made the importing of anything from England, France or their territories illegal. By the time the restriction on West Indian molasses was lifted, Bourbon and Rye Whiskies had supplanted rum as the settler's favorite.

51. How is Rum made?

When the sugarcane (grows from 6 to 20 feet high) is ready for harvest, it is chopped down either by hand or by mechanical harvester. The stalks are brought into the sugar mills, to the distillery where they are shredded and the sugar-laden pulp is crushed by heavy rollers. The juice (known as *vesou*) is collected, strained, decanted, and filtered. There are many ways in which distillers produce rum and there is no one method that all distillers use. Generally, the juice is boiled to evaporate the water, which crystalizes the sugar and then clarified with the aid of a centrifuge, which separates it from the residue...molasses. The juice inoculated with yeast and fermented, producing a small amount of alcohol, and then distilled or double-distilled in *pot stills* or *continuous stills* to below 190 proof. Dark, full-bodied rums are usually distilled in pot stills at a lower proof (140–160), maintaining much of the flavor components in the final distillate. It is estimated that it takes about 1.5 liters of molasses to make one liter of rum

52. Aging
There are no internationally agreed legal definitions or "standards" of aging. Each country may or may not impose aging requirements for rum production.

Both light and dark rums come out of the still colorless, although they may taste quite different. Light (or gold) rums are generally kept in glass or stainless steel tanks, but occasionally wooden barrels. Dark (full-bodied) rums are aged in charred oak barrels previously used for Bourbon and Cognac, or uncharred barrels from Sherry wine.

53. Añejo Rum
Virtually every rum producer also makes a high-quality, well-aged rum, which is sometimes labeled as *añejo*.

However, there is no requirement as to how old rum has to be to be designated *añejo*. Most *añejo* rums are aged more than a couple of years, although a few are not, and may be colored with caramel for effect.

Classifications of Rum

There are four major styles of rum: light (or gold) rum, dark (full-bodied) rum, Demerara rum, and *rum agricole*. The above styles (in addition to flavored or spiced rums) are made in many countries, each with its own style, production methods, and flavor.

54. Light (or Gold) Rum

Light rum is clear in color and displays either a very light, molasses flavor or the neutrality of vodka. It is aged in either glass or stainless steel containers, but more traditionally is aged in uncharred barrels. If aged in barrels, it is further treated through carbon filtration systems, which eliminate any color that may have been picked up from the barrel. Gold rum, also labeled "amber" rum, is either aged in wooden barrels or colored by the addition of caramel. Light rum is also labeled *white, silver,* or *platinum.*

55. Dark (Full-Bodied) Rum

Rum that derives some of its color from aging in charred oak barrels. Dark rum is fuller in body, obviously darker in color, and dominated by more complex caramel and butter notes, rather than the simple suggestion of sweetness in most light rums. Dark rums may be distilled twice in pot stills and aged for years prior to release; this darkens the spirit but the final color is almost always achieved by adding caramel.

56. Demerara Rum
Often high-proof, dark-colored rums produced from molasses and sugarcane grown along the Demerara River in British Guyana, South America. Demerara rums are some of the darkest of rums, but the rum is rather light-bodied, lighter in flavor than most Jamaican rums. Demerara rums are delicate and fruity, occasionally flavored with fruits and spices and aged for more than a decade. Some Demerara Rums used to be shipped to London for aging, which were then labeled "London Dock Rums." In years past, Demerara Rums were often consumed by lumberman and fishermen in far northern climates, who drank it half-and-half with hot water as *grog* to warm the bloodstream. *See* Turbinado Sugar.

57. Rum Agricole
Rum made from fresh sugar cane juice, which is fermented into alcohol. Rum made from sugar cane juice is also known as *rhum agricole* and *agricultural rum*, whereas rum made from molasses is also known as *industrial rum*. Countries where rum agricole is produced include Guadeloupe, Haiti, and Martinique.

Styles of Rum by Language

58. Spanish-Speaking Islands
Traditionally produce light rums with a fairly clean taste and delicate features, with hints of molasses. Rums from Colombia, Cuba, Dominican Republic, Guatemala, Nicaragua, Panama, Philippines, Puerto Rico, and Venezuela are typical of this style.

59. English-Speaking Islands
Traditionally produce darker, fuller rums with a fair amount of molasses. Rums from Antigua, Bahamas, Barbados, Bermuda, Jamaica, St. Croix, and the Virgin Islands are typical of this style.

60. French-Speaking Islands
Traditionally make fuller-bodied rum from sugarcane juice, with an aroma and flavor that is herbal, vegetal, and grassy, with hints of molasses. Rums from Guadeloupe, Haiti, and Martinique are typical of this style.

Other Important Terminology

61. Babash
An extremely potent, locally produced overproof rum with a fearsome reputation produced in Trinidad. It is generally sold under-the-counter (illegally) and usually

available during sugarcane harvest time. Babash translated means *bush rum.*

62. Batavia Arrack

A high proof, distilled spirit made on the island of Java (Indonesia) since at least the early seventeenth century. The combination of the special quality of the river water on the island of Java and the addition of the dried red Javanese rice cakes that are added to the mash during fermentation results in the highly aromatic and flavor of this rum. The rice cakes are placed into sugarcane molasses, which then ferments naturally. The distilled rum is aged about three years in Java and then shipped to Holland where it is further aged for up to six years before being blended and bottled. Batavia arrack is also known as *aromatic rum.*

63. Clairin

A very strong, clear, unaged rum-type distilled spirit, historically used in Voodoo ceremonies in Haiti.

64. Grog

A name for a rum drink derived from the nickname of Vice Admiral Edward Vernon (1684–1757), the English naval officer for whom George Washington's estate, Mount Vernon, was named. The admiral was known as "Old Grog" because he wore a shabby boat coat made out of *grogram,* a coarse fabric woven from silk and wool and often stiffened with gum. While anchored at Port Royal, Jamaica, on August 21, 1740, he ordered that henceforth, the crew was to drink a daily ration of a half-pint of rum, mixed with hot water, sugar, and lime juice, as a caution against scurvy. This practice ended on July 31, 1970 and was referred to as Black Tot Day. On September 1, 1862, the United States Navy passed an act declaring that rum rations given to sailors while at sea should be abolished. (The rum, known as Royal Navy Rum was 95.5 proof.) Grog is also known as *Navy Grog* (England).

65. Jamaican Rum
A dark, full-bodied, pungent rum, distilled from molasses and used mostly in cocktails.

66. Monkey Rum
A distilled spirit made from the syrup of the *sorghum* plant. It has been produced in North Carolina since the 1920s, although some suggest it has been made as early as 1899.

67. Pimento Dram
A dark-colored, medium-sweet, spicy hot liqueur made in Jamaica, from a base of rum with infused allspice (clove, cinnamon, and nutmeg).

68. Rum Fanny
A round tin container once used by the Royal Navy for the service of rum. The container, which previously

contained mutton rations, was named after Fanny Adams, an 8-year old girl, who was the victim of a notorious murder in 1867. A sailor, finding a button in a tin, suggested that it probably came from the coat of Fanny, which led to the use of the name *Fanny* to describe such tins of meat.

69. Rum Liqueur
A liqueur bottled at not less than 60 proof, in which the distilled spirit used is entirely rum, and that possesses a predominant characteristic rum flavor derived from the distilled spirit used.

70. Splice the Mainbrace
An old Navy term given aboard vessels to issue the crew a drink (rum). The term appears in some of Herman Melville's writings. The term refers to the *brace* (a rope used to hold direction of the sail) attached to the main yard of a sailing ship. The *mainbrace*, being one of the heaviest pieces of rigging equipment on a sailing ship would generally not be *spliced* if damaged, but rather replaced. However, if damaged at sea, the brace would have to be spliced very quickly, because the ship was unable to be effectively steered.

71. Tafia
The name given in the early 1700s, by inhabitants of French-speaking islands in the Caribbean to low-quality

rum generally made from impure molasses or other sugarcane residue.

72. What is Flavored Rum?

According to U.S. federal regulations (1992), flavored rums are a mixture of distilled spirits that are flavored and colored with various types of fruit and/or herbs and may or may not contain added sugar. Some flavors are apple, banana, blackstrap molasses, cherry, citrus, coconut, coffee, lemon, lime, mango, melon, orange, passion fruit, peach, pineapple, raspberry, spiced, and vanilla, plus others. They are bottled at not less than 60 proof (30 percent alcohol by volume) and the name of the predominant flavor *must* appear on the label.

73. Some Brands of Rum
American-Made:

Crusoe, Owney's

Imported:

(Anguilla): Pyrat; (Antigua): Bambu; (Austria): Stroh; (Barbados): Cockspur, Malibu, Mount Gay, The Real McCoy; (Bermuda): Gosling; (British Virgin Islands): Pusser's; (Colombia): Ron Medellin, Ron Viejo de Caldas; (Cuba): Havana Club; (Dominican Republic): Atlantico, Barceló, Brugal, Kirk and Sweeney, Ron Matusalem, Vizcaya; (Guatemala): Montecristo, Ron Zacapa; (Guyana): El Dorado; (Haiti): Rhum Barbancourt; (Jamaica &

Guyana): Sea Wynde; (Jamaica): Appleton, Montego Bay, Myers's, Wray & Nephew; (Martinique): Kaniche, Rhum Clément, Rhum St. James; (Mexico): Puerto Angel; (Panama): Malecon, Ron Abuelo; (Philippines): Tanduay; (Puerto Rico): Bacardi, Caliche, Captain Morgan, Don Q, Palo Viejo, Ron Castillo, Ron del Barrilito, Ron Llave, Ron Rico; (St. Croix): Cruzan; (Trinidad & Tobago): Kraken Black Spiced Rum, Old Oak, Zaya; (Trinidad): Angostura, Caribbean Club, Fernandes, Forres Park, Royal Oak; (U.S. Virgin Islands): Conch Republic; (Various Countries): Admiral Nelson, Banks, Trader Vic's, Whaler's; (Venezuela): Diplomatico

74. Popular Cocktails

Bacardi, Banana Cow, Blue Hawaii, Bounce, Caipiriñha, Calibogus, Champoreau, Copacabana, Cuba Libre, Daiquiri, Eggnog, Flip, Hot Buttered Rum, Hurricane, Long Island Ice Tea, Mai Tai, Mary Pickford, Milk Punch, Mojito, Pimento Dram, Piña Colada, Planter's Punch, Rompope, Rum & Coca-Cola, Rumrousal, Shrub, Sling, Stone Fence, Switchel, Tom & Jerry, Zombie

75. Serving and Storing Rum

With the exception of well-aged rum, white, gold, and dark rums are best enjoyed in cocktails, usually containing coconut milk, pineapple juice, or the juice of citrus fruits.

Rum is an extremely versatile beverage that can be substituted in most cocktails calling for gin or vodka and occasionally even tequila. Rum, like gin, vodka, and tequila, is a highly stable alcoholic beverage that is not adversely affected by vibrations or changes in temperature; in most cases, it will last indefinitely, either opened or unopened.

Well-aged rums should be given the same treatment as brandies or cognacs; they are served in brandy snifters at room temperature.

76. What is Cachaça (kah-SHAH-sah)?
An alcoholic beverage fermented and distilled in Brazil from pure sugarcane juice and is essentially white rum.

77. History & Background
It is believed the word *cachaça* is a translation of an African term for liqueur. Many believe that cachaça production began soon after the introduction of sugarcane into Brazil––sometime around 1550. Whether it was accidentally or intentionally, sugarcane juice fermented, thereby producing alcohol. Eventually, someone realized that distilling the fermented cane juice made it a more potent potable and, cachaça was born. It was in 1610 in the city of São Vicente in the State of São Paulo that the production of cachaça began. In the days of sailing ships, the captains of many vessels would often

stop at Rio de Janeiro for repairs, fresh water, and a supply of cachaça as a replacement for their crew's "rum ration." For centuries, cachaça was produced almost exclusively for natives, sailors, and the lower classes. Cachaça became the drink of the locals and alcoholism quickly spread. The Brazilian elite regarded cachaça as a poor man's drink, preferring instead imported wines, whiskeys (scotches) and cognacs. In the late nineteenth century with the influx of foreign capital and modern distillation equipment, the once floundering industry began to produce high-quality cachaça, which became the drink of fashionable Brazilian nightclubs.

78. Aging
Aging is not required, but Brazilian law stipulates that cachaça must be aged at *least one year* to be labeled *aged.* Aging generally takes place in used bourbon whiskey or Madeira wine barrels, or locally produced *amburana, amendiom, balsam, freijó, jequitibá,* and *vinhático* wooden barrels.

79. Some brands of Cachaça
Agua Luca, Cachaça 51, Cachaça 61, Cachaça da Roça, Leblon, Pirapora, Pitú, Ypióca

80. Recommended Cocktail
Caipiriñha (*kai-pee-reen-yah*) Cocktail (translated means "a little countryside drink.")

"They make this drink in Brazil called Cachaça. It's sugarcane alcohol. Costs 35 cents a quart. One quart of that stuff and you see God. Two quarts and you grow a pair of tight pants and an electric guitar." (Van Halen's David Lee Roth, *June 1984*)

Tequila (Mezcal, Bacanora, Sotol, and Tlahuelompa)

"Tequila. Straight. There's a real polite drink. You keep drinking until you finally take one more and it just won't go down. Then you know you've reached your limit." (Lee Marvin, American actor)

81. What exactly is Tequila?

Tequila is a distilled spirit made from a fermented mash (juice and/or sap) derived principally from a blue variety of the genus plant *Agave tequilana Weber* (named in 1902, by Franz Weber, a German botanist, from earlier work begun in 1896), with or without additional fermented substances. (The leaves of this species of agave are tinted blue.) Tequila is NOT made from cactus!

82. Country of Origin

By government decree (1976), tequila can only come from a specific geographic area of Mexico known as Tequila, which is within the state of Jalisco and in parts of the states of Guanajuato, Michoacán, Nayarit, and Tamaulipas. If produced outside these geographical limits, it is may be called *mezcal*. Tequila gained its own denomination of origin in 1997. Jalisco is approximately 4,260 feet above sea level and due to its proximity to the sun; the agave plants mature quicker and have more concentrated sugars. As a result of the concentrated sugars, these plants are highly sought after for the production of tequila. The soil in Jalisco is mineral rich, red clay that retains moisture and warmth of the sun, creating a unique style of tequila that is somewhat drier and more acidic.

83. What is the History & Background of Tequila?

The ancient Aztec Indians, around 900 B.C., despite having no distillation knowledge or equipment created an alcoholic beverage called *pulque*, by fermenting the juice of agave plants. The first *tequila-type* beverage was produced by Hernando Cortéz (1485–1547), in 1519, who conquered Mexico and brought with him the art of distillation. In 1653, settlers founded the town of Tequila, which continues as the center of Mexico's tequila production.

84. Laws & Regulations

Norma Oficial Mexicana (NOM) In an effort to control the production and quality standards of tequila, the Mexican government devised a set of strict regulations. These standards (usually referred to as *normas*) specify what tequila is and how it must be made. Each distillery that adheres to production methods set down by law is given its own NOM number, which is required to be placed on the label. This number is not a guarantee of quality, merely authenticity. These regulations were formerly known as *Dirección General de Normas* (DGN).

85. What is Agave?

A huge plant, indigenous to Mexico, southwestern United States and central and tropical South America.

There are more than 136 species, having stiff, often-spiny leaves and prickly, needle-like thorns, resembling cactus. The agave plant is a relative of the lily. Each plant grows five to eight feet tall and eight to twelve feet wide and takes eight to twelve years to reach full maturity. The heart of the agave plant weighs between 75 to 175 pounds and contains what the distiller calls the sap or *aguamiel* (honey water). The agave plant is sometimes known as *American aloe, century plant*, and *maguey*.

Labeling

There are two principal types of tequila depending on the amount of agave used during the fermentation process. "100 Percent Agave Tequila" and "Mixto Tequila."

86. "100 Percent" Agave Tequila

Indicates that all the fermentable sugars were derived from agave. These tequilas are generally labeled "100 percent Blue Agave" or "100 percent Agave." If it doesn't say 100 percent agave on the label—it isn't. Tequila made from 100 percent blue agave may not be and must be bottled within the designated areas of production in Mexico (2005).

87. Mixto (Blended) Tequila

Tequila that is made from a mixture of minimum 51 percent blue agave and other sugars such as cane, corn syrup, molasses or other unrefined sugars. The addition of sugar lowers the cost of producing tequila, but also lowers the quality. Mixto production began in the 1930s because of an increase in demand for Tequila and a limited harvest of agave. Prior to this all were 100 percent blue agave. *Mixto* Tequila may be shipped in bulk to the United States for bottling.

Piloncillo is unrefined brown sugar, made from dried sugarcane, often used in the making of *mixto tequila*, to speed fermentation.

88. Types of Tequila

Tequila can be grouped into four distinctive categories—Blanco, Reposado, Añejo, and Extra Añejo.

Blanco Tequila: An unaged Tequila bottled after proofage reduction by distilled water no longer than 60 days after distillation. Blanco Tequila is also known as *plata Tequila* and *silver Tequila*.

Gold (or Oro) Tequila: *A sub-group of blanco Tequila.* A straw-amber colored, unaged Tequila that has been treated with caramel to give the appearance of wood aging. Gold Tequila, which is a *mixto* Tequila, cannot be aged beyond 60 days. The caramel gives the tequila a rounder, fuller, and softer feel in the mouth, with some slight sweetness. This Tequila is often referred to as *joven abocado* (Mexico).

Reposado Tequila: "Rested Tequila." Tequila that has been aged in oak barrels (previously housed Bourbon, Cognac, Scotch, or Burgundy wine) for a minimum of 60 days and a maximum of one year. However, in practice, they are aged from two to 11 months. There is no regulation for *reposado* Tequila to be made from 100 percent agave.

Añejo Tequila: Tequila that has been aged for a minimum of one year and a maximum of three years in oak barrels (some aged longer) not exceeding 600-liters. There is no regulation for *añejo* Tequila to be made from 100 percent agave.

Extra Añejo Tequila: Tequila that is aged for a minimum of three years in oak barrels (some aged longer) not exceeding 600-liters. There is no regulation for *extra añejo* Tequilas to be made from 100 percent agave. This classification took place on October 28, 2005.

89. Other Terminology.

Agavero: One who grows or *farms* agave plants used in making Tequila and mezcal.

Aguamiel: The sticky sap (or *honey water*) released from the agave plant, used in making Tequila or mezcal. Children often consume this honey water. *See* Pulque.

Autoclave: A large stainless steel *pressure cooker* used to steam the *piñas* used in the making of Tequila.

Blue Agave: A variety of the genus plant *Agave tequilana Weber* (named in 1902, by Franz Weber, a German botanist, from earlier work begun in 1896), which has blue tinted leaves. This is only agave that can be used to make Tequila. Blue agave is also known as *agave azul*.

Caballito: A narrow shot glass containing 1 to 2 ounces, modeled after a hollow bull's horn, which is what Spanish colonists used to drink Tequila. The name translates to mean *little horse*.

Century Plant: A name incorrectly given to the agave plant by early pioneers in the Southwestern United States, because it was mistakenly believed to bloom only once every 100 years. Actually it takes about 10 years or so in warm regions and as much as 60 years in colder climates to bloom. Century plant is also known as *American aloe*.

Fábrica: A factory, plant, mill, or distillery, where Tequila is produced.

Hijuelo: The *baby* agave or offspring taken from the mother plant and replanted to grow into a mature agave plant, to be used in making Tequila.

Horno: The traditional stone or brick ovens used to *cook* agave *piñas* in the making of Tequila.

Limón: A light green citrus fruit with a taste quite similar to lemon and lime, with the flavor of lemon predominating. It is indigenous to Mexico and the southwestern United States, where it is traditionally served with Tequila drinks. Although limes are the customary citrus fruit used in the United States for margaritas, lemons offer a more authentic taste.

Mezcalero: A distillery that makes mezcal.

Molineros: Distillery workers in charge of the *tahona* and grinding-mashing process in the making of Tequila and mezcal.

Pencas: The spiky, thick leaves of an agave plant, used in making Tequila and mezcal.

Pulque: A viscous, milky-white alcoholic beverage fermented (not distilled), with an earthy, herbaceous flavor, is produced from the juice of agave plants. Pulque was enjoyed for centuries by the Aztecs before the art of distilling came to Mexico from Spain. Because of its rather low alcoholic content (4 to 6 percent) and susceptibility to spoilage, it is consumed locally and rarely reaches the United States. The nonalcoholic version of pulque, called *honey wine* is often consumed by children. *See* Aguamiel.

Tequilero: One who makes tequila.

Tahona: A heavy (approximately two tons) stone wheel used to crush the agave *piña* in the making of Tequila and mezcal. Donkeys, oxen, horses, or tractors turn the stone. Tahona is also known as *molino* and *noria*.

90. Does a bottle of Tequila contain a worm?

One will occasionally hear of a person finding a worm (*gusano*) at the bottom of a bottle of tequila. In fact, the worm is not found in bottles of tequila, only certain bottles of mezcal. The worm, which is actually the larvae of the Mexican night butterfly, which infests overripe agave plants, has no real significance other than tradition and a shrewd marketing gimmick. Supposedly, Jacobo Lozarto Paez invented this practice in the 1940s and 1950s.

There are many stories of how the worm came to be introduced into bottles of mezcal. One is that, in the old days, with no scientific aids to determine the alcohol content of the finished product, placing the worm in the mezcal would establish the alcohol content. If the worm pickled and was preserved, the mezcal was good. If the worm decayed, the mezcal had to be re-distilled.

91. What is Flavored Tequila?

According to U.S. federal regulations (1992), flavored tequila is a mixture of distilled spirits that are flavored and colored with various types of fruit and/or herbs and may or may not contain added sugar. Some flavors are almond, coconut, cinnamon, kiwi, lemon, lime, mango, orange, pear, pineapple, quince, strawberry, tangerine, vanilla, and watermelon, among others. They are bottled at not less than 60 proof (30 percent alcohol by volume) and the name of the predominant flavor *must* appear on the label.

92. Some Brands of Tequila

1800, 4 Copas, Agavero, Asombroso, Avión, Cabo Wabo, Cabrito, Campo Azul, Cancun, Casa Noble, Casco Viejo, Centinela, Chinaco, Corazón, Corralejo, Corralejo, De Los Altos, Don Diego, Don Emilio, Dorado, El Conquistador, El Cuate, El Diamante del Cielo, El Mayor, El Tesoro, El Toro, Espolon, Frida Kahlo, Gavilan, Gran Centenario, Gusano Rojo, Herradura, Intrigue Suave, José Cuervo, Juarez, La Arenita, Lapiz, Los Arango, Margaritaville, Milago, Monte Alban, Montezuma, Oro Azul, Patrón, Pedro Domecq, Pepe Lopez, Sauza, Sol Dios, Tenoch, Tézon, Tonala, Torada, Torado, Tres Rios, Two Fingers

93. What does Tequila taste like?

Silver

Aroma and flavor of: black pepper, dill, earthy, grape-fruit, grassy, green apple, green olive, herbaceous, lemongrass, lime, pine, sage, tobacco, vegetal, and wet cement. Blanco has a natural affinity to salt and lemon juice.

Reposado

Aroma and flavor of: black pepper, caramel, cocoa, dried grass, figs, smoke, tobacco, toffee, vanilla, vegetal, wet stone, and white chocolate.

Añejo

Aroma and flavor of: butterscotch, caramel, cinnamon, citrus, dark chocolate, dried fruit, ginger, honey, maple, nutmeg, orange, pepper, smoky, toasty, toffee, and vanilla.

94. A Tequila Ritual.

The standard ritual for drinking straight tequila consists of—first wet the fleshy area between your thumb and index finger, sprinkle salt on the wet spot, and then "lick" the salt with your tongue. Immediately follow with a straight shot of tequila, downed in one gulp. Then put a lemon wedge into your mouth and suck deeply. This ritual is known in Mexico as *Los Tres Cuates*—"The Three Chums."

95. Popular Cocktails

Long Island Iced Tea, Margarita, Sangrita, Tequila Sunrise, Topless Margarita

96. Are there any songs about Tequila?

- On December 23, 1957, The Champs, a vocal group, recorded the song "Tequila."
- In 1973, the song Tequila Sunrise was written by Don Henley and Glenn Frey and recorded by the Eagles.
- In 1977, singer, song-writer, Jimmy Buffett recorded the song "Margaritaville."
- In 1983, country vocalist, Shelly West recorded the song, "Jose Cuervo."

97. What is Mezcal?

A *tequila-like* alcoholic beverage produced in the state of Oaxaca (outside the Tequila zone), south of Jalisco, an area rich in Aztec history. Mezcal can also be produced in the states of Durango, Guerrero, San Luis Potosi, and Zacatecas. Most mezcal is made from several types of agave, unlike tequila, which is made from the *Tequilana*-blue agave. The agave is often cooked in underground ovens with wood charcoal fires, giving mezcal a somewhat smoky smell and taste. Traditional aging was in cured, large black clay ceramic jugs called *cantáro*. Mezcal must be double-distilled, but may be triple-distilled.

In 1995, a law was passed protecting the name Mezcal with an *AOC*, from being made from anything except approved agave plants. The law classified Mezcal into two categories: Type I: 100 percent agave, usually handmade in small batches. Type II: A minimum of 80 percent agave (compared to 51 percent for *mixto* tequila). On the label its written "Bottled in Origin," whenever it's bottled in the producing state, while mezcal bottled outside one of the producing states must be labeled "Bottled in Mexico." Also spelled *mescal*.

98. Aging Categories for Mezcal

Blanco or Joven: Bottled immediately after distillation.

Joven Abocado: The addition of coloring agents to the mezcal.

Reposado or Madurado: Aged a minimum of two and a maximum of 12 months in wooden barrels.

Añejo: Aged a minimum of one year in wooden barrels, no larger than 200-liters.

99. What is Bacanora?
An agave-based distilled spirit coming from the state of Sonora, which was made illegal in 1915 (legalized in 1992). In 2000, the Official Gazette of Mexico published the "General Declaration of Protection to the

name Bacanora." The declaration states that Sonora is the only state in which the production of Bacanora is acknowledged. Bacanora has been made for more than 300 years and is produced from agave grown high in the mountains, which is roasted over mesquite fire in underground pits. The roasted agaves cores are removed, chopped, and allowed to ferment. Bacanora is double-distilled in a copper pot stills and bottled at 40 percent alcohol by volume.

100. What is Sotol?

A regional form of mezcal made from the *sotol* plant, which has large thorns on serrated leaves, similar to agave. It is produced in the northern state of Chihuahua, but is native to the states of Durango and Coahuila. The Tarahumara and Apache Indians fermented a drink from syrup similar to pulque. The Conquistadors later distilled this liquid and it became known as *sotol*. Sotol can only be made from 100 percent sugars from the sotol plant.

101. What is Tlahuelompa?

An agave-based distilled spirit coming from the state of Hidalgo, made from fermented blue agave syrup.

"One tequila, two tequila, three tequila, floor." (George Carlin)

DRINKS OF AMERICAN PRESIDENTS
AND FAMOUS PEOPLE

"The three-martini lunch is the epitome of American efficiency. Where else can you get an earful, a bellyful, and a snootful at the same time?" (Gerald R. Ford 1913–2006, American president)

Presidents

- Abraham Lincoln: Didn't Drink
- Andrew Jackson: Bourbon Whiskey, Rye Whiskey, Vermouth
- Andrew Johnson: Bourbon Whiskey, Rye Whiskey
- Benjamin Harrison: Didn't Drink
- Bill Clinton: Beer, Gin & Tonic
- Calvin Coolidge: Tokay Wine, Gin

- Chester A. Arthur: Wine, Liqueurs
- Dwight D. Eisenhower: Scotch Whisky, Eggnog, Bourbon Whiskey
- Franklin D. Roosevelt: Old-Fashioned, Gin Martini (Plymouth Gin), Bourbon Whiskey, Scotch Whisky, Beer, Brandy, Rum, Manhattan
- Franklin Pierce: Many Different Beverages
- George H. W. Bush: Vodka Martini, Beer
- George W. Bush: Doesn't Drink
- George Washington: Madeira, Champagne, Rye Whiskey, Porter Beer
- Gerald Ford: Gin & Tonic, Martini, Beer
- Grover Cleveland: Beer
- Harry S. Truman: Bourbon Whiskey, Old-Fashioned Cocktail
- Herbert Hoover: Wine, Dry Gin Martini
- James A. Garfield: Scotch Whisky (Dewar's), Beer
- James A. Madison: Wine, Champagne
- James Buchanan: Champagne, Cognac; Madeira, Sherry, Rye Whiskey
- James K. Polk: Wine, Champagne, Brandy
- James Monroe: Rum, Champagne, French Red Wine
- Jimmy Carter: White Wine
- John Adams: Rum Punch, Beer, Hard Cider, Porter, Madeira
- John F. Kennedy: Daiquiri, Bloody Mary, Heineken Beer, Scotch Whisky, Gin Martini
- John Quincy Adams: Madeira, Wine, Beer

- John Tyler: Mint Julep, Champagne
- Lyndon B. Johnson: Cutty Sark Scotch Whisky
- Martin Van Buren: Sherry; Whiskey, Schiedam Gin
- Millard Fillmore: Madeira Wine
- Richard M. Nixon: Scotch Whisky, Château Margaux, Rum & Coke, Dry Martini, Sparkling Wine
- Ronald Reagan: BV Private Reserve, Vodka & Orange Juice
- Rutherford B. Hayes: Didn't Drink
- Theodore Roosevelt: Sherry, Mint Juleps, Hot Milk Punch, Brandy, Rum
- Thomas Jefferson: Wine, Champagne
- Ulysses S. Grant: Bourbon Whiskey, Champagne, Rum Punch
- Warren G. Harding: Whiskey
- William Henry Harrison: Hard Cider, Bourbon Whiskey, Eggnog
- William Howard Taft: Champagne, Gin
- William McKinley: Rye Whiskey, Sweet Vermouth, Cherry Brandy, Absinthe
- Woodrow Wilson: Scotch Whisky
- Zachary Taylor: Whiskey

Famous People

- Alfred Hitchcock: Plymouth Gin
- Ava Gardner: Whiskey, Gin
- Benjamin Franklin: Madeira Wine, Hard Cider

- Buddy Hackett: Gin Rickey
- Daniel Webster: Old Crow Bourbon
- Dean Martin: Scotch Whisky, Martini
- Dorothy Parker: Champagne Cocktail, Martini
- Dylan Thomas: Whiskey
- Edgar Allan Poe: Brandy, Gin
- Edgar Degas: Absinthe
- Edouard Manet: Absinthe
- Ernest Hemingway: Absinthe, Beer, Rum, Gin, Daiquiri, Martini, Wine
- Eugene O'Neil: Gibson
- F. Scott Fitzgerald: Gin Rickey, Martini
- Frank Sinatra: Jack Daniel's, Bourbon Whiskey, Martini, Scotch Whisky
- George Bernard Shaw: Whiskey
- George Burns: Martini
- George Lucas: Martini
- Hank Williams: Whiskey
- Henry Clay: Old Crow Bourbon
- Humphrey Bogart: Scotch Whisky, Martini
- Ian Fleming: Plymouth Gin
- Jack Benny: Martini
- Jack Kerouac: Martini
- Jack London: Old Crow Bourbon, Martini
- Jackie Kennedy: Château Pétrus (In Addition To Other Bordeaux Wines)
- James Joyce: Wine
- J. K. Rowling: Gin & Tonic
- John Barrymore: Whiskey

- John D. Rockefeller: Martini
- John Wayne: Sauza Conmemorativo Tequila
- Johnny Carson: Martini
- Judy Garland: Vodka
- Lucius Beebe: Champagne, Jack Daniel's
- Marilyn Monroe: Champagne (Piper-Heidsieck)
- Mark Twain: Old Crow Bourbon Whiskey
- Mae West: Martini
- Oscar Wilde: Champagne, Absinthe
- Orson Welles: Scotch Whisky, Negroni Cocktail
- Pablo Picasso: Absinthe
- Philip Marlowe: Gimlet
- Queen Elizabeth II: Gin &Dubonnet
- Raymond Chandler: Whiskey, Gin Gimlette, Martini, Stinger
- Richard Harris: Vodka
- Robert Benchley: Martini, Orange Blossom
- Stephen King: Beer
- Tennessee Williams: Ramos Fizz
- Tony Curtis: Vodka
- Truman Capote: Screwdriver
- Walt Whitman: Old Crow Bourbon Whiskey
- William Faulkner: Whiskey, Mint Julip, Jack Daniel's
- William S. Burroughs: Vodka & Coke
- Winston Churchill: Scotch Whisky (Johnnie Walker), Brandy, Plymouth Gin, Pol Roger Champagne, Cointreau, Martini, Highball, Red Wine (Claret)

Frank Sinatra: "Let me fix you a Martini that's pure magic." Dean Martin: "It may not make life's problems disappear, but it'll certainly reduce their size." (From the film *Some Came Running*, starring Frank Sinatra and Dean Martin, 1959)

QUOTES—VODKA, GIN, RUM, & TEQUILA

"A man must defend his wife, his home, his children, and his Martini." (Jackie Gleason, 1916–1987, American comedian)

"A small carafe of vodka, very cold," ordered James Bond. (Ian Fleming, Casino Royale, 1953)

"A well-dressed gentleman seated at the bar was quietly guzzling martinis. After finishing each one, he carefully ate the glass and arranged the stems in a neat row. The ninth time this occurred, the bartender could stand it no longer and commented to another customer, There's a guy who's absolutely nuts. He sure is, agreed the other man. The stems are the best part." (Author Unknown)

"Art for art's sake makes no more sense than gin for gin's sake." (William Somerset Maugham, 1874–1965, English short-story writer, novelist and playwright)

"Before drinking a martini, should you eat the olive first or last? First; growing up I was told it's not healthy to drink on an empty stomach." (Bob Lipinski)

"Call me what you like, only give me some vodka." (Russian Proverb)

"Do not allow children to mix drinks. It is unseemly and they use too much vermouth." (Steve Allen, 1921–2000, Television and radio personality)

"Gin. A modern nickname for the liquor called geneva or genevre. The Epithet Royal is affixed to it, because, when beggars are drunk, they think themselves as great as kings." (Bailey's Dictionary, 1720)

Gin Lane

"Drunk for a penny,
Dead drunk for twopence,
Clean straw for nothing!"
(A sign painted in 1750, by William Hogarth, an English barkeeper, which hung above a Shoreditch grog-shop and depicted squalor and degradation.)

"There is something about a Martini,
A tingle remarkably pleasant;
A yellow, mellow Martini,
I wish that I had one at present.
There is something about a Martini,
Ere the dining and dancing begin,
And to tell you the truth,
It is not the vermouth—
I think that perhaps it's the gin." (Ogden Nash, 1902–1971: *A Drink with Something in it,* 1935)

"Gin-drinking is a great vice in England, but wretchedness and dirt are greater." (Charles Dickens 1812–1870, *Sketches by Boz,* 1836)

"Happiness is a dry martini and a good woman—or a bad woman." (George Burns 1896–1996, U.S. actor and comedian)

"Happiness is...finding two olives in your martini when you're hungry." (Johnny Carson, 1925–2005, American television host and comedian)

"Have you got any good gin, sir? Yes, sir, Hollands. Well, mix me a cocktail—I want to wet up." (Sir James Edward Alexander, *Transatlantic Sketches*, 1833)

"Hearts full of youth, hearts full of truth. Six parts gin to one part vermouth." (Tom Lehrer 1928–, American folk singer, *Bright College Days*)

"How reckless of me. I made you all wet. Yes, but my Martini is still dry." (James Bond and Fatima Blush, *Never Say Never Again*)

"I doted on the cool, refreshing scent of a good saloon on a hot summer day." (H. L. {Henry Louis} Mencken, 1880–1956, American writer, *Happy Days*, 1940)

"I drink martinis the way other people take aspirins." (Imbibing them at lunch and dinner until he was well into his eighties) (Elwyn Brooks "E. B." White, 1899–1985, American writer, *New Yorker Magazine*)

"I think I had it in the back of my mind that I wanted to sound like a dry martini." (Paul Desmond, 1924–1977, sax player in the *Dave Brubeck Quartet*)

"I'm not talking a cup of cheap gin splashed over an ice cube. I'm talking satin, fire and ice; Fred Astaire in a glass; surgical cleanliness, insight...comfort; redemption and absolution. I'm talking MARTINI." (Author Unknown)

"I'm tired of gin. I'm tired of sin. And after last night, oh boy, am I tired." (Author Unknown)

"If it wasn't for the olives in his martinis he'd starve to death." (Milton Berle)

"Let us candidly admit that there are shameful blemishes on the American past, of which by far the worst is rum." (Bernard DeVoto, 1897–1955, American Writer)

"Let's all drink gin and make wry faces." Wally Campbell (Bob Hope, *The Cat and the Canary*, 1939)

"Martinis…have a muting effect on the constant ringing in my ears, and as five o'clock approaches, my thoughts turn toward the elixir of quietude. Gin stops the bell from tolling." (Elwyn Brooks "E. B." White, 1899–1985, American writer, *New Yorker Magazine*)

"Once the pleasantries are over, the powerful discuss deals over Martinis." (Bob Lipinski)

"One martini is all right. Two are too many, and three are not enough." (James Thurber, 1894–1961, *Cartoon Caption* New Yorker Magazine)

"Perhaps it's made of whiskey and perhaps it's made of gin, perhaps there's orange bitters and an orange-peel within, perhaps it's called Martini and perhaps it's called again, the name that spread Manhattan's fame among the sons of men; perhaps you like it garnished with what thinking men avoid, the little blushing cherry that is made of celluloid, but be these matters as they may, a *cher confrere* you are if you admire the cocktail they pass across the bar." (Wallace Irwin, *The Great American Cocktail*, San Francisco, News Letter, March 8, 1902)

"That other supreme American gift to world culture, the martini, will do only at its own hour." (Bernard DeVoto, 1897–1955, American Writer, The American Spirits, *The Hour, Chapter 1*)

"The martini is a city dweller, a metropolitan. It is not to be drunk beside a mountain stream or anywhere else in the wilds, not in the open there or even indoors." (Bernard DeVoto, 1897–1955, American Writer, *The Hour*)

"The only American invention as perfect as a sonnet." (When referring to a martini). (H. L. {Henry Louis} Mencken, 1880–1956, American writer)

"The purest of all spirits." (When referring to gin) (André L. Simon, French wine writer, 1877–1970)

"There aren't any ugly women, only too little vodka." (Old Polish Saying)

"There is a point at which the marriage of gin and vermouth is consummated. It varies a little with the constituents, but for a gin of 94.4 proof and a harmonious vermouth it may be generalized as about 3.7 to one." (Bernard DeVoto, 1897–1955, American Writer, *The Hour, 1946*)

"There is no such thing as a one martini." (John Doxat, book author)

"There's naught, no doubt, so much the spirit calms as rum and true religion." (Lord Byron "George Gordon Noel Byron," 1788–1824, English poet, *Don Juan*)

"There's truth in wine, and there may be some in gin and muddy beer; but whether it's truth worth my knowing, is another question." (George Eliot, *Felix Holt*)

"They say a martini is a like a woman's breast; one ain't enough and three is too many." (Gale the cocktail waitress {Doria Cook-Nelson], *The Parallax View*, 1974)

"We shall drink to our partnership. Do you like gin? It is my only weakness." (Doctor Pretorius "Ernest Thesiger" *The Bride of Frankenstein*, 1935)

"We tell our employees not to drink or cuss when they're on the job, but we also tell them that if they're going to drink on the job, they should make it scotch or bourbon, not vodka, so the clients will know they're drunk, not stupid." (Harry Carter)

"When I have one martini, I feel bigger, wiser, taller. When I have a second, I feel superlative. When I have more, there's no holding me." (William Faulkner, 1897–1962, Author)

"Whiskey's too rough,
Champagne costs too much,
Vodka puts my mouth in gear.
This little refrain
Should help to explain
As a matter of fact I like beer." (Tom T. Hall, 1936–, American country music singer)

"Who could visualize the world before 1860, a world in which the day Martini had no place? It must have been a bleak and arid earth that lacked the frosty, limpid, and luminous brew that today transforms the weary, work-laden executive into a sparkling and rejuvenated companion, or makes the child-bound housewife feel, for one evening hour, like a queen." (J. A. [James Anstruther] Maxtone Graham, *Book Author*)

"You can no more keep a martini in the refrigerator than you can keep a kiss there. The proper union of gin and vermouth is a great and sudden glory; it is one of the happiest marriages on earth, and one of the shortest-lived." (Bernard DeVoto, 1897–1955, American Writer, *Harpers Magazine, December 1949*)

"Zen martini: A martini with no vermouth at all. And no gin, either." (P. J. O'Rourke, 1947 -, Political satirist, journalist, and author)

54241680R00077

Made in the USA
Lexington, KY
07 August 2016